COCKFIGHTING

COCKFIGHTING

Solving the Mystery of
Unconscious Sabotage at the
Top of the Corporate Pyramid

ISABELLE NÜSSLI

LEVERAGE YOURSELF AG

COCKFIGHTING
Solving the Mystery of Unconscious Sabotage
at the Top of the Corporate Pyramid

ISBN   978-1-5445-1311-9 *Paperback*
            978-1-5445-1310-2 *Ebook*

To everyone who is tired of unnecessary conflict
and wants to do something about it.

To all the bad experiences that turned out to be great ones.

CONTENTS

INTRODUCTION...9

PART I: THE DRIVERS OF CONFLICT

1. THE CEO/CHAIRPERSON RELATIONSHIP 23
2. THE CONSCIOUS ELEMENTS OF CONFLICT........................37
3. THE UNCONSCIOUS ELEMENTS OF CONFLICT.....................49

PART II: THE INTENSIFIERS OF CONFLICT

4. BIRTH ORDER..67
5. LACK OF SELF-AWARENESS 85
6. TOXIC COMBINATIONS...95

PART III: THE TOOLS TO PREVENT AND MITIGATE CONFLICT

7. IMPROVE SELF-AWARENESS...115
8. CREATE A COLLABORATION CONTRACT 143
9. ADVICE FOR UNDERSTANDING DIFFERENT BIRTH
   ORDERS IN THE WORKPLACE..159

CONCLUSION..167
ACKNOWLEDGMENTS 175
ENDNOTES 177
REFERENCES 181
ABOUT THE AUTHOR 193

INTRODUCTION

At a fairly young age, I was thrust into a role that most people do not fill until much later in their career: I was invited to serve as chairperson of a leading international provider of event infrastructures. The company belonged to my husband's family, and the year ahead of us showed every sign of being a historic one, with several high-profile contracts—the FIFA Soccer World Cup in South Africa, the Winter Olympics in Vancouver, the World Exposition in Shanghai, India's Commonwealth Games, and the World Equestrian Games in Kentucky. Despite my youth, I was confident in my experience—I had already built up the company's US business, as well as established and run their global Key Account Management program. In addition, my solid management education from the Kellogg School of Management suited me well for leading the thriving family business's board of directors, and I was excited by the opportunity.

As chairperson, I led our company's search process for a new CEO. After five months, we found a person that seemed to be the right fit. He brought great qualifications to the role, along with a promising mix of personal charm and go-getter spirit. However, his transition into the role was not easy. He had a habit of repeating, "I'm the boss," to workmates. The deeper he became involved in organizational politics, the more his focus seemed to drift away from solving the issues we'd brought him in to address. Instead, he recommended that we change the organizational rules and functional charts to give him more sway over the organization. I spoke to him more than once about the need to course-correct, but to no avail. In such moments, his professional demeanor seemed to switch into a more personal mode. He responded by urging my family to sell its majority share in the business and "go enjoy life."

This took me by surprise, to say the least. Who says something like that to their superior? But as the months progressed, it became unmistakable that, for this CEO, power seemed very important. After twenty months, we parted ways.

Shortly thereafter, all hell broke loose. A newspaper got

hold of the story of his departure and reported that the reason behind it was his poor job performance. I can only imagine how displeased our former CEO must have felt to see this negative press. Two weeks after that first article came out, we woke up to articles full of misinformation and slander about the company, the board of directors, and the family. The final straw came when our former CEO started his own company, nearly identical to ours in purpose and scope, and quickly began hiring away key employees from our company.

After much turmoil and unrest, with the help of a good turnaround manager and a strategic acquisition, our company managed to weather the storm without losing any contracts or clients. However, it was a tumultuous time, both physically and emotionally. I was left with so many unresolved questions. I could not fathom how a person would act in that manner or go that far to achieve and hold on to power, especially in the face of what we thought were clear corporate governance rules. I thought I knew about ambition, politics, and power games, but this was nothing I'd seen or heard of before. But I also spent a lot of time questioning my own actions and behavior, trying to see how I might have contributed to the conflict. What could I have done better or differently?

As I spoke with other people in senior corporate positions,

however, I learned that I was far from alone. The majority of people in executive leadership had experienced similar issues, particularly in the context of CEO/chairperson relationships. I couldn't believe so many people had suffered similar emotional and professional turmoil and, moreover, had never spoken about it. It seemed that admitting problems of this nature and magnitude was viewed as taboo—tantamount to an admission that their leadership, business, management, or personal power structures were weak.

MY AHA! MOMENT

Time passed, and eventually our family sold the company. I continued to ponder these events. I embarked on a master's degree in international business law at the University of St.Gallen, seeking to learn how a company's legal framework brought together hard law with the "soft law" of corporate governance. With clear rules in place that set standards for company roles and functions, I wondered, how was there still so much conflict, especially among top leaders with decades of leadership experience behind them?

As I read and reflected, I began to get a glimpse of something more profound, more personal, behind the machinations of leadership that neither law nor corporate governance could explain. That something was the human element. While the business world is constructed as a rational system, its practical functions are rife with irrational behavior. To understand it, I would have to go outside the bounds of business law and management theory and delve into human psychology.

This "aha!" moment culminated in an executive master's degree in consulting and coaching for change at the business school INSEAD. Rather than being all about formal structures and rational functions, the program focuses on the human element in business: What happens when people interact in business settings? How does it play out? Why do teams and processes work? Why do they not work?

While I was still writing my thesis for my law degree, INSEAD approved my application and invited me to join their program. While it was not my plan to pursue two master's degrees at the same time, I felt it was an opportunity I just had to take. It turned out to be one of the most inspiring journeys of my life. Over the course of two years, we learned about ourselves and human beings in general, discovering strengths, weaknesses, and most importantly, the behavioral patterns that define professional relationships. Through this work, we learned how to lead others in overcoming patterns, relaxing their defenses, and harnessing their potential for the good of their careers and their companies.

I had to write a second thesis for the completion of the program. Based on my past experience and the insights received from my network, I decided to focus on the CEO/chairperson relationship. This research effort proved the theory I had been pulling together ever since my experience with my former CEO: most relationships between CEOs and chairpersons do not function well. Politics and power games run rampant in the highest tiers of organizations, creating a climate of frustration, exhaustion, and mistrust. My research also revealed a common denominator: behavior patterns predominantly could be traced back to family upbringing. The roles and expectations imprinted on a person during childhood, along with a series of conscious and unconscious drivers, solved the mystery of why these leadership conflicts derail as badly as they do.

My work in this program made everything else I had learned and experienced about business, international business law, and corporate governance fall into place. I had many unanswered questions about why top leadership relationships work the way they do. The missing piece was right in front of me. The clearly documented parameters of corporate governance fall short where people's subconscious comes into play. But understanding those patterns—and where they come from—holds hope for real change.

A BETTER WAY IS POSSIBLE

Cockfighting is a very strong title, referring to the bloody (and illegal) sport where two animals with a natural instinct to compete for dominance are trained to fight each other until one is seriously wounded or dead.

This scenario provides an apt metaphor for the conflict that often occurs between two strong personalities. Like cockfighting, the co-leader conflict comes from a deep instinct that is cultivated by the high-pressure atmosphere of a corporate environment. Like cockfighting, this instinct can be encouraged by society, which tends to place leaders on a pedestal, thus motivating them to compete for distinction. And like cockfighting, the conflict often ends with leaders harming themselves as well as each other.

Today's business world moves at breathtaking speed, with ever-increasing demands on leadership. Facing intense pressure not only from outside competition but also from within organizations, senior leaders often feel increasingly overwhelmed, and at the same time unwilling to betray any hint of vulnerability to their co-leaders or colleagues. This pressure brings to light all sorts of fears and doubts that interfere with engagement and productivity, especially when combined with power games and conflicts among fellow leaders.

When psychological suffering is this intense, it cannot simply be left at the office. It bleeds out into every aspect of an executive leader's life, causing problems with family, chronic health issues, or a growing sense of despair and isolation. As their constant effort grinds against a mounting sense of hopelessness, far too many leaders never reach out for help, convinced that this level of stress and conflict is normal—an unfortunate but unalterable aspect of working within the upper echelon of business management.

However, they could not be more mistaken. Business does not have to be this way.

THE KEY TO REAL CHANGE

This book is based on over seventy interviews with CEOs and chairpersons in and from different countries and organizational cultures, both public and private, large and small, along with the insights I've gained from my ongoing practice as a leadership coach and my personal business experience. In addition to my degrees in business, law, and applied business psychology, I've held senior management positions in international businesses. In 2017, I founded my own leadership platform, Leverage Your Self, which offers coaching and consulting to everyone from board members to management teams to start-ups, helping them use psychological insights to tap into their potential and overcome the pressures of today's business climate in order to thrive professionally and personally.

Not all relational conflicts are bad—the business world often presents leaders with conflicts that ultimately help a company improve and grow. However, 95 percent of the leaders I interviewed perceived that the majority of relationships between chairpersons and CEOs do not work well. When relationships are bad, especially between executive leaders, the conflicts they generate are counterproductive and can be ultimately destructive, both to the individuals involved as well as to the company as a whole.

In these pages, you'll find tools and concepts that can help improve relationships between chairpersons and CEOs, as well as between and within executive teams and boards of directors. As these relationships improve, so does a company's culture, productivity, and performance. It is not rocket science. A substantial part of these benefits stems from establishing successful, high-functioning relationships. While circumstances vary by organizations, at the end of the day, it comes down to how human beings function in relationships, especially where power is an element.

Most people have a basic awareness of the behavioral patterns that they manifest within a conflicted relationship. However, they often have little understanding of where these patterns come from and, even more importantly, how to overcome them. To create that deeper understanding, it is essential to start from a foundation of nonjudgment. None of the patterns we bring from our family background and upbringing are inherently good or bad. They are just there. The key is getting to know them and choosing how to redirect those patterns in a way that serves us better.

Admittedly, the process of cultivating deeper awareness is not always comfortable. However, it is a crucial component of personal development that guarantees not only an improved work environment, but also enhanced job performance, company productivity, career prosperity, and psychological well-being—and it also benefits personal life. In short, it is work worth doing. Moreover, it can even be fun.

START FROM WHEREVER YOU ARE

You may be currently caught in the toxic spiral of a CEO/chairperson conflict, you may simply have the sense that your leadership relationship is headed in a negative direction, or you may be on the verge of walking out the door on a relationship that is past saving. No matter where you find yourself, my hope in writing this book is to show there is another option. By cultivating self-awareness around your own behavior patterns, you can improve your professional well-being and contribute to a better environment for everyone in your workplace.

Best of all, improvement does not have to rely on your leadership counterpart to commit to cultivating the same awareness. As you learn about the conscious and unconscious drivers behind your behavior, the specific intensifiers that trigger your behavior, and the individual aspects of your upbringing, you will learn how to use these elements to bring out your best qualities, abilities, and traits, and bring them out in those you lead and your leadership counterpart. You will gain a comprehensive understanding of how to create, maintain, and nurture healthy relationships with yourself and others.

As you learn to create better relationships within your professional life, that ability will extend into your personal, social, and family life, ultimately generating a profoundly positive impact on your overall well-being. Progress is addictive. In time, you will find increased joy in educating and coaching others in your workplace by sharing your insights with them.

It is common to regard a stressful, conflict-laden situation as being someone else's fault—to assume that if everyone else involved in a conflict would change their behavior, everything would be fine. But by using the principles in this book to gain more control and insight into your own behavior patterns, you'll be able to change situations by changing your own response.

The ultimate goal of mastering these principles is to thrive in your job. As you make these changes, those in your environment cannot help but notice. As your ability to thrive improves, your engagement, productivity, creativity, and ultimately your performance will also improve, creating a trajectory of progress that will take you farther than you ever would have been able to go before.

PART I

THE DRIVERS
OF CONFLICT

CHAPTER 1

THE CEO/CHAIRPERSON RELATIONSHIP

Understanding the tensions that exist between a chairperson and a CEO starts with understanding the descriptive meanings of these two leadership roles. There are many different definitions that I could have used to define these two roles, but I chose a dual interpretation process known as Interpretive Phenomenological Analysis, or IPA.

This process relies on asking subjects to share stories that give meaning to their world, then decoding those stories through a psychodynamic lens to make sense of the phenomenon. In my research sessions, this meant interviewing CEOs and chairpersons with an extensive series of questions, some structured and some open-ended, customized to suit each individual's experience and elicit their perspective on the relationship with their leadership counterpart. Then, rather than rely on my own interpretation of their responses, I worked with each interviewee to help them interpret their experience.

Despite the deeply personal nature of these interviews and their duration (an average of two hours per session), I was able to collect a large sample group. Within twenty-four hours of reaching out to the first sixteen candidates, I had an appointment with fifteen of them, which reflected both trust and a high interest in the topic. My interviewees came from a diverse range of perspectives—males and females, ages forty to sixty-six, coming from both current and former CEO/chairperson positions, from both publicly traded and private companies, representing industries including hospitality, real estate, finance, telecommunications, energy, consumer goods, and others. It was undeniable that the CEO/chairperson relationship was a hot topic, and no case more clearly defined the tension of this relationship than that of Bob and James.

BOB VERSUS JAMES

Bob was the CEO of a company, while James was its chairperson. During their last board meeting, both men left the boardroom in a fury after Bob announced a plan of acquisition.

In this situation, as CEO, management respon;
entirely within Bob's purview. Managemen
bility is with him, the CEO, and his team, an‹
task to propose the strategies that the board of directors
decides on. The board's job is to supervise and monitor.
James's repeated involvement in the daily business is a
clear overstepping of his role, at least as Bob sees it. He
has considered resending James their company's function chart of organizational rule to remind him of the
corporate governance system.

James, of course, knows these rules very well and is, himself, considering whether to tighten their constraints to
curb Bob's new habit of waiting until the board meeting
to present critical plans. In James's book, that is a violation of Bob's role. As chairperson, James, along with
his board, bears the organization's utmost responsibility
and liability. He is Bob's boss, and as such, needs to be
informed fully and on time about business operations.

Both leaders feel their position is the more powerful one,
which results in a tug-of-war for authority. Bob has the
advantage of greater on-the-ground presence within the
business's daily operations, while James's influence over
the board gives him a say in Bob's job security.

If this dynamic continues unchanged, what happens to
these two leaders? What happens to the company and

the employees in it? One possible situation is that Bob is able to convince the board that he is too important to lose and maybe even influence the shareholders to restructure the board. The more likely scenario, however, is that Bob gets fired. If he goes on withholding information from the board and influencing the management team, the board may lose trust in him and dismiss him.

In that case, James would have to hire a new CEO. While James could take the opportunity to carefully vet new candidates for compatibility of personalities and leadership styles, a more likely scenario is that he chooses someone weaker than Bob and grooms him or her to be what he wants in a CEO, i.e., someone who does not oppose his involvement in business operations.

In the less frequent case, if Bob gets to stay and receives a say in the selection of a new chairperson, he would likely act similarly to choose someone who doesn't oppose him.

Still, too often new CEOs are hired because the board either wants different personalities or little mini-mes working for them. They seldom look at compatibility and the potential for a true partnership, and thus, they only learn about their counterpart's personality traits when the pressure is on and power and money are involved. Under pressure, role overlap becomes more apparent and conflicts arise. This is when role clarity and the conscious and unconscious elements that drive conflicts become crucial. A CEO has to have a healthy respect for authority, and a chairperson must not get entangled in daily business.

TODAY'S TENSIONS WORSENING

Back when life seemed a little simpler—before digital disruption, demographic changes, and the accelerated pace of innovation—it was more common for leaders to single-handedly run a company. In many ways, it made organizational operations more efficient—one person was trusted to have all the answers, and leadership unilaterally went top-down.

Today, however, the world turns much faster. With increasing dependencies on a dizzying array of factors—technology, social media, artificial intelligence, as well as globalization and geopolitical concerns—that seem to change from one day to the next, demands on leadership have increased. It is much harder for one person to have all the answers. Forced to shoulder more pressures than ever before, leaders are faced with the necessity of working more collaboratively.

This makes personality as key to successful leadership as expertise. Leaders' personalities influence the people around them, the culture, and ultimately the performance of the company. But while this seems obvious, personality is not often a key factor in hiring top leaders. Instead, CEOs are predominantly hired on the basis of rational requirements. Such a portfolio says little about someone's emotions or motivations, much less about their compatibility or chemistry with existing leadership. It makes no sense to hire someone within a vacuum when they will not work within a vacuum. What drives them? Money? Success? Appreciation? It is hard to tell until it is experienced. If not assessed up front, often these important aspects and drivers are not learned until the relationship fails.

In the case of a leadership relationship failure within a public or well-known company, the company will spin it as a different understanding in terms of strategy misalignment, or opposing leadership styles. Take ABB, a Swiss multinational corporation that operates in robotics, power, heavy electrical equipment, and automation tech. The day after the company decided to sell off much of its financing portfolio, their then-CEO, Jörgen Centerman, resigned, and the then-chairperson, Jurgen Dormann, took over as CEO. The company put out a statement about Dormann taking over in order to "speed up effective implementation of the company strategy." Dormann also stated that the former CEO decided to step down himself after he found out that fresh new blood would be in the company's interest.

According to Centerman's statement in the press, his decision to step down was entirely due to a personal conflict with the chairperson, a pure relationship issue. Within a week of being named CEO in 2001, he wanted to restructure 160,000 employees and was quoted as saying, "I want to leave my own footprint."[1] Centerman was cited to hold his title as a badge of pride, while Dormann would make statements like "CEOs are 'dangerous animals'"[2] that need to be kept in line.

Dormann also said something quite ambiguous about Centerman, to the effect of, "He smelled morning air, but it was the wrong perfume. Let's leave it that way."[3] What he presumably meant was the CEO got a sniff of too much power.

Another example comes from the Swiss lingerie manufacturer and seller Calida. A conflict between a longstanding CEO and two parties—the founding family as the largest shareholder and the board of directors—came to light in terms of strategic development. The CEO wanted to continue acquisitions and conquer challenging market conditions, while the board and family wanted to focus on organic growth. Later, the media wrote that the difference between them was not just in terms of strategy, but, as the chairman stated, because of a break of trust since the CEO divulged confidential information to the public.

THE FALSE COMFORT OF THE RATIONAL

Along with strategy misalignment, a common cover for transitions of power in high management positions is to cite differences in leadership styles or the CEO's intention to retire, followed by messages such as "thankful for their service" and the CEO is "looking forward to spending more time with family." When they name a successor in the press, both the board of directors and the leaving CEO express their confidence that the new CEO is "the right person to lead the company going forward." Most of the time, the story that isn't put out to the public is that there were relational conflicts. In either case, the careful use of boilerplate language emphasizes a rationale behind the confusion that ensues when leaders part ways. Business culture prefers to deal with a clear right and wrong. Interpersonal dynamics and psychology are considered irrational, even "fluffy"—corporate governance, by contrast, seems rational and reliable.

There are currently controversial discussions taking place around the topic of combining leadership roles as a solution for co-leader conflict. However, there seems to be little empirical evidence that combined leadership roles are better or worse for future performance or governance quality. The advantages and disadvantages of each structure depend on the situation. The question of whether to separate might be the wrong one to ask. Instead, it should be asked how the two leaders at the top can improve and nurture their relationship for the benefit of company culture, productivity, and ultimately performance.

Refusing to acknowledge psychological and relational issues only leaves defensive mechanisms in place to deal with them. But while it is much easier for a company to focus on company law and on corporate governance to define guidelines, mechanisms, and procedures by which corporations are controlled and directed, these rational elements continually fall short in preventing and resolving conflict. This is not because they are not strictly binding and thus cannot be enforced, but mainly because they are rational—they do not take human behavior into account.

The late Wayne Calloway, the former CEO and chairman of PepsiCo, Inc., who was frequently featured in magazine lists of most admired CEOs, recognized this fact decades ago: "I'll bet most of the companies that are in life-or-death battles got into that kind of trouble because they didn't pay enough attention to developing their leaders."[4]

As long as humans have been around, telling us what the rules are does not change our behavior in a profound way. It just makes us find more creative ways of justifying or bending rules to better serve ourselves. Laws can be interpreted and applied in ways to support an agenda. The irrational is always present, but it is not really examined, leading to decades of conflicts and scandals that even corporate governance has fallen short of avoiding and dealing with.

Still, too many people go through their day-to-day looking at others' flaws without really understanding or taking responsibility for their own actions or impulses. At the top levels of a company, conflicts are usually about power and other irrational aspects.

THE PSYCHOLOGICAL CONTRACT

Not all agreements between people are transactional. Just as often, agreements are relational, formed without verbal expression or written documentation. This is the nature of a psychological contract. Conceptualized in the 1960s by organizational psychologist Dr. Chris Argyris and popularized by organizational psychologist Dr. Denise Rousseau in the 1990s, the psychological contract perfectly describes an employment relationship. While transactional contracts are short term, have a specific duration, and deal with extrinsic aspects, relational contracts are objective, longer term, broader, and focused on intrinsic factors. They also require a high personal commitment to fulfill.

Few people realize joining a company means immediately entering into a psychological contract. While your transactional contract is with the company itself, so is your psychological contract, theoretically. But because an organization cannot be part of a contract, it is predominantly formed with the person at the other end of the table, who personifies the organization for you. For a CEO, this is the chairperson. For the chairperson, this is the shareholders or the directors of the board. Each of these individuals comes to the table with their experience, expectations, and a belief in an obligation of reciprocity.

Psychological contracts say a lot about the attitude and behavior of a person, in that they refer to expectations of promised exchanges. You expect to give something, and, in return, you expect to receive something. This contract is breached when one party perceives that the other has failed to fulfill its promise and is violated when strong emotional reactions are triggered. This is negatively linked to job performance, satisfaction, and commitment.

The psychological contract is based on experience and is completely subjective. Thus, when the contract is perceived to be violated, it elicits a strong emotional reaction. For example, you might feel betrayed, angry, resentful, or experience a decreased level of trust. These perceptions are influenced by your upbringing, experience, and personality.

Usually, people are unaware of their psychological contract with an organization or, as a representative of the former, with a person. It happens unconsciously. This is why trust is so key to maintaining a healthy psychological contract. Lack of trust is linked with inferior quantity and quality of communication and cooperation. It is also related to problem-solving and performance in a negative way.

Again, in the rational context of corporate governance, there's an embedded sense that trust doesn't play a factor. Duties and responsibilities are laid out in a black-and-white agreement. If you do what you are supposed to do, you stay or get promoted; if you do not, you get reprimanded or fired. But trust works beyond those transactional relationship.

For trust to develop, people need to spend time together. The chairperson is usually not full-time, so trust is harder to gain. The more comparable psychological contracts are between the chairperson and the CEO, the higher the stability of the relationship.

INNER THEATER

There are lots of hidden factors and drivers that shape a person's attitudes toward, and perceptions of, others. These may stem from trust or distrust, confidence or insecurity, close communication or secrecy. According to Dr.

Manfred Kets de Vries, clinical professor of leadership development and organizational change at INSEAD,

> Each employee has his or her own "inner theatre," a program that each individual has incorporated from both nature and nurture...This inner theatre is a product of genetic inheritance and childhood experience. The interplay between the two leads to highly complex motivational need systems...Each individual carries these mental schemas...throughout life.

For example, the way a person related to his or her caregivers during the first years can determine how this person will relate to others as an adult. This script of life, or how you experience and internalize childhood, also leads to patterns that define expectations of others' responses and how you react to them. Very often, this script becomes unproductive in adulthood.

Luckily, these behaviors are not set in stone. The key lies in recognizing how your past has shaped your present. This is where awareness comes into the picture. Nobody is immune to the drivers of impulses and emotion, but as Manfred Kets de Vries points out, psychological awareness is the first step to psychological health.

It is important to remember that conflicts are more common than you might think. The way we deal with them is not all about rational aspects; it is more about the irrational and intangible. Companies and media do not usually examine this aspect of relationships. The good news is that something can actually be done about it. Both the parties to the relationships and third parties witnessing or being negatively affected by the relationship can contribute to its improvement, via self-development or helping others improve.

Sure, it can be challenging, but so is business. The family origins, past experiences, and life-changing incidents that shape us do not make us better or worse. They simply form the unique portfolio that each of us has to deal with. Regardless of what yours might look like, thriving in a leadership context requires making a concerted effort to do something productive with it.

CHAPTER 2

THE CONSCIOUS ELEMENTS OF CONFLICT

A conscious driver of conflict is a dynamic in the relationship that you are aware of. You recognize it as something that impacts your behavior. If someone were to ask you why the relationship works or does not work, a conscious driver will usually come to your mind right away, though, like the leaders I interviewed, you may not know why it appeared or how to manage it.

In addition to conscious drivers, there are a number of unconscious drivers of conflict. We will explore these in the next chapter.

TRUST

Throughout my interviews, when CEOs and chairpersons were asked what makes the relationship with their co-leader work, the overwhelming majority of answers came down to one word: trust.

In just the first twelve interviews, the word was mentioned over forty times. It was used to describe negative relationships as well as positive ones—"I cannot work with him because he does not trust me" versus "Our relationship works because we trust each other." Despite the reliance on corporate governance within the workplace setting, personal reflection led top-level leadership to openly acknowledge trust as the most powerful factor in their co-leader relationship.

At the same time, however, these leaders were not completely aware of how to manage trust.

With trust established as the most powerful conscious driver of conflict in their co-leader relationship, the question remains of how trust can be built and cultivated. According to Denise Rousseau, two conditions lead to trust: judgment of integrity and belief in benevolence. However, everyone has their own relationship with trust and recognizes it intuitively.

Trust is crucial for a healthy psychological contract.

Lack of trust is linked to inferior quantity and quality of communication and cooperation. Building trust forms togetherness, provides security, and influences people's interpretations of social behavior.

Most interviewees stated that they give people the benefit of the doubt, but immediately after, added that they need to see proof of action. This is an interesting dilemma because trust takes time to be built, but they were expressing an immediate need for it.

Stable patterns of interaction are important for predictability and trust building. Clear and open communication and avoiding surprises are key. Surprises actually undermine stability. Most leaders mentioned a breach of trust or unmet expectations as the reasons for tensions or conflicts. In actuality, they had *perceived* breaches. They would say things like "I was promised the chairperson role, but I wasn't given it," or "The chairperson always sets the competencies," or "The CEO only told me about the acquisition in the board meeting." These psychological contracts are made unconsciously and, when not met, erode trust. For this reason, it makes sense that trust is possibly the most powerful conscious driver of conflict in the co-leader relationship.

Along with trust, two other conscious drivers of conflict presented themselves during my research with CEOs and chairpersons. These two conscious drivers that emerged were role clarity and role models/anti-role models.

ROLE CLARITY

Roles within a company are largely defined from the outset, either within a job description or through roles assigned to someone when they take on a task. This is the "what" of the role. However, the "what" is always informed by the "how," or the individual's perceptions of what a role means and what it requires of them.

Leaders will always bring their own personality, emotions, capabilities, and history into play when interpreting and fulfilling roles. On top of this, roles tend to overlap among people, the system, and context—in other words, few roles exist in a vacuum. When people hold different perceptions around a role, it can trigger negative feelings, reduce an individual's satisfaction with the role, and create conflict.

A common mistake leaders make in this regard is conflating role with identity. Leaders tend to bring a history of role assumptions into their position. This so-called role biography is the sum of each role that the person has held in the past, starting with their childhood and leading into their current role, and encompasses assumptions that unconsciously affect the person's thoughts, feelings, and behaviors within the role. But also the role in a system has a history. It is not neutral. The stronger and more effective the role itself is, the higher its influence on the holder of the role. This is called "role history."

When someone becomes too attached to their role and title, they are unable to step back and look at themselves as separated from the role—to do so feels like a threat to their identity and their personal power, as well as the power of their position. But when roles are separated from identity, people tend to act and make decisions for the betterment of the company, employees, and shareholders.

Finding congruence between roles and others' expectations is complex territory. Every CEO or chairperson role comes with certain expectations attached to it, simply by nature of it being at the top level of leadership. Congruence triggers positive feelings and a continuation of the same behaviors, entailing a reinforcing cycle, while incongruence creates negative feelings, misunderstandings, and dissatisfaction, which might lead to erratic decision-making.

For this reason, every role would benefit greatly from co-leaders discussing not only the specific responsibilities of the role but also the relationship dynamics around it—the question of expectations versus definitions. Like any contract, the clearer a psychological contract can be, the better. What prevents a lot of people from doing this is the assumption that they already know how to fulfill the role. Others assume that it is their co-leader's responsibility to claim role clarity, but are then dissatisfied when that person's idea does not match their own.

A CEO might walk into a role thinking they need to lead with a strong hand because they have their own history of observing and acting out the role. They also have a perspective and expectations of their counterpart's role. The CEO might think he knows exactly what he needs to do and how he wants to fill his role, but the same set of conditions holds true for his counterpart, the chairperson. If the two do not sit down and talk about these roles, expectations, and perceptions for themselves and each other, how could their relationship possibly go smoothly?

ROLE MODELS

Fifty percent of the leaders I interviewed cited specific authority figures from their past who serve as their conscious guide for how they fulfill their own leadership roles.

A role model may have been a positive or negative force in their life, a kind or unkind authority figure—depending on this experience, the person makes a conscious decision to imitate or to oppose this model. These models were usually someone close to them and who was their senior in some sort of way, be it age or career-wise. In many cases, these authorities were primary caregivers or superiors from previously held positions. While a positive role model prompts a person to say, "I always aspired to be a strong leader like my first boss," a negative role model might provoke a reaction like "I had a horrible chairperson when I was CEO at X company, and I swore I'd never act that way if I became a chairperson in the future."

While role models/anti-role models can be useful in fostering an individual's leadership ethics, they can become drivers of conflict when the consequences of a role model or anti-role model oppose the co-leader's value system or interpretations based on his past experience.

The presence of role models impacts the psychological contract between co-leaders. If a CEO, for example, sees an unkind role model in his or her chairperson who serves as their contract maker, it can negatively impact their relationship. While the same holds true on the positive side, many interviews revealed a definite bent toward the negative: one-fourth of all individuals (two-thirds of them were CEOs) I interviewed saw current or past chairpersons as anti-role models. This affected their belief in the obligation of reciprocity in their present co-leader relationship.

THE GOOD, THE BAD, AND THE UNKIND

Rami and Vinish, chairperson and CEO respectively, had a bad relationship. They ran into conflict beyond just the discussion of roles and handing out organization rules for corporate governance. Because they never explicitly discussed their individual power relative to each other, they constantly jockeyed for it. Rami, the chairperson, played the authority card, while Vinish played with the power of withholding information. Rami said he was the boss and needed all the information. He would constantly keep pushing and exert his authority over the CEO.

Vinish thought he only had one way to exert his power and fight back. He knew everything about the business and chose to withhold certain information in order to exert his power.

They didn't discuss their job descriptions or what they meant in terms of their actions relative to one another. Instead, they relied on their personal understanding of their roles and handed out rules accordingly. Both needed to better understand how to handle the potential overlap of roles. Their relationship struggles created a toxic environment that impacted everyone around them and affected the working atmosphere, productivity, and ultimately the company's performance.

On the other side, we have Vicky and Ian, chairperson

and CEO respectively, who took the time at the outset of their working relationship to actually discuss their roles in detail. Vicky left a past position as CEO of another company due to conflicts with her former chairperson, who always interfered with Vicky's decisions about daily operations. When she assumed the role of chairperson at Ian's company, Vicky initiated a discussion with him about expectations around each of their roles, so that they would both be up front and clear about where each of them figured in the context of the business. For Vicky, this discussion made her feel confident and secure in her position—the respect Ian showed for her authority engendered reciprocity in their psychological contract. For Ian, the discussion felt liberating—with expectations clearly defined, he could focus on the business, the market, and the clients without having to play politics with someone. Both went into their co-leader relationship with an incredibly positive energy that filtered down to the company employees and boosted morale and performance.

Role models can be good for one person in the relationship, while for the other person it comes across negatively. Take the case of chairperson Chris, who thrives on structure and order. During his interview, Chris shared that his father's untimely death created a huge ordeal for his whole family—he had to spend a lot of time and effort cleaning up the mess of documents and financial matters that were left. This left Chris with the conviction that strict structure is the only way to ensure the consistent, reliable order essential to running and passing on a business successfully. At a deeper level, maintaining this strict order gives Chris a sense of security that he is performing his role well.

For this reason, Chris finds it very important to be transparent about the division of power, and he communicates about it frequently to ensure that his CEO, Patrick, hears and understands him. For Patrick, however, this constant emphasis on structure and order translates as a mania—to him, Chris comes across as obsessive and micromanaging. For that reason, Patrick often withholds information from Chris about daily business operations, because it is the only way he sees to retain power in his own position. Neither of them realizes that in lieu of playing this power game, they could learn to understand and respect each other's style of leadership.

Another case involves Kelly and Nicki, who had a good relationship primarily because Kelly, as chairperson, did her utmost to stick to her responsibility as a chairperson and never step on the toes of Nicki, her CEO. In a former company, Kelly had served as CEO under a chairperson who always tried to steal her spotlight. After struggling to do her job and fighting for the respect she deserved, she promised herself that if she ever became a chairperson, she would do things differently.

When she became chairperson at this new company, it was scary at first for her not to intervene more often, because she was afraid she would give her CEO too much space. But as you might guess, Nicki regarded Kelly's style of nonintervention with great appreciation. By practicing trust and respect with her CEO, Kelly received that trust and respect right back.

AWARENESS (ALONE) IS NOT THE ANSWER

The nature of conscious drivers makes this issue more mysterious. After all, if CEOs and chairpersons are aware of these obstacles standing in the way of a successful relationship, why do they remain in conflict?

The answer is simple: an individual's awareness of an issue does not necessarily mean they can do anything about it. Even when both parties know they have divergent interpretations of their role definitions and expectations, and experience the conflict that results, their ability to address these issues is influenced by many things they have no control over.

In other words, rationality does not solve everything. As the next chapter will show, there are a lot of hidden, unconscious elements and their intensifiers at play in the co-leader relationship such as upbringing, power (im)balance, time spent together, birth order, and self-awareness, all of which influence a person's psychological contract and fuel irrational, unproductive behavior. These unconscious drivers are the real forces running the show, engendering unpredictable behavior. Successful leadership cannot be arbitrated by charts, definitions, or rules alone—the oft-neglected human element needs to be taken into account and discussed.

CHAPTER 3

THE UNCONSCIOUS ELEMENTS OF CONFLICT

David grew up as the youngest in a family of older siblings. At the time that his brothers and sisters were going through puberty, he was ten years younger, unequipped to deal with the boundary-pushing and the fighting around the dinner table that fractured the family's harmony. The discomfort he felt from this conflict led him, at age eleven, to propose a deal with his parents. He told them he wouldn't cause any trouble if they let him "do his thing" throughout his teenage years. His parents accepted his proposition, and it worked out well for everyone in his family.

That same deal, however, has not worked out as well in David's professional life, especially once he assumed the role of CEO. In fact, the deal he struck with his parents prevented him from honing the skills needed to deal with conflict. As a result, David admits his policy at work is to avoid conflict, sometimes to an unhelpful degree. While his conflict-avoidant nature makes him popular among the employees he manages, it has been an obstacle in his relationship with his chairperson. He tends to default to a "you are the boss" position in negotiations with his co-leader. He does not always stand up for himself, even when he feels strongly about an issue. David realizes this behavior is directly tied to his upbringing among anti-role models and family dynamics.

George, like David, was a younger child among much older siblings. As the baby of the family, he usually had no idea what his older siblings and parents were talking about at the dinner table. He felt excluded and overlooked during these "adult discussions." Consequently, at a young age, George promised himself that he would make his own footprint rather than simply follow the same path in life as his siblings. As a result, he became very entrepreneurial, starting little businesses selling things to family members and neighbors. It very much led to the way he conducted himself in his adult life, finding his own way of approaching and implementing business matters and, if he feels they are threatened, defending them.

Many leaders give little to no thought to their upbringing when reflecting on the experiences that shaped their professional life—they tend instead to look back only as far as their first job. But upon digging deeper, they begin to realize how much their upbringing shaped their value system and how, in turn, a certain work atmosphere caused them to react a certain way, from their first jobs to their current positions.

George and David were no different. Despite being initially uncomfortable with talking about their upbringing, looking at their childhood helped them see how the value systems they grew up with—particularly the ones that caused them pain and confusion—led them to form opposing approaches to their behavior as adults in the workplace.

DEFINING UNCONSCIOUS DRIVERS OF CONFLICT

When interview participants were asked why their co-leader relationships were not working well, none of them cited unconscious factors as a possible reason. Part of this is because of the very nature of unconscious drivers—they are not obvious. In addition, however, people (especially in the business world) tend to deny or downplay the presence of unconscious processes, even when they constantly live them out through behaviors and actions. In general, they do not like to think their behavior is controlled by anything other than the rational mind.

FAMILY UPBRINGING

Time and again, family upbringing consistently proves to be the first and one of the strongest unconscious drivers of conflict in CEO/chairperson relationships.

Research confirms that family upbringing shapes personality, which in turn shapes the way people develop their own values and habits of behavior. It also shapes psychological contracts, the perception of contract breach, and responses to these perceived breaches. A person's present environment mainly serves to interpret and reinforce the knowledge gained through early childhood experiences.

TRANSFERENCE

When leaders were asked whether their counterparts, CEOs, or chairpersons, reminded them of someone from their past, they mostly said no. However, when given time to reflect or consider examples of others' experiences, these same individuals would amend their statements. It was almost as if they unconsciously needed permission to access these models in their memory. Their hesitancy makes sense—sharing stories is, after all, an act of trust. Once trust was built through both my sharing of stories and their learning about another leader's vulnerability, they became more open to being vulnerable in discussing childhood experiences and how they impacted their daily lives.

Therefore, a second major unconscious driver of conflict is transference, first described by Sigmund Freud. To quote psychiatry professors Dr. Burness E. Moore and Dr. Bernard D. Fine, who defined this term in the 1990s, "Transference is a displacement of patterns of feelings, thoughts, and behavior originally experienced in relation to significant figures during childhood onto a person involved in a current interpersonal relationship." In the business organization context, that means employees act toward their leader as though they are an important authority person from their childhood. In doing so, they unconsciously project dreams and emotions onto that person. This can result in an employee acting in accordance with prior behaviors, but it can also result in them defying prior behavior patterns and acting in ways they wish they had.

Transference impacts a psychological contract much like role models and anti-role models do. The outcome can be positive or negative, depending on the feelings and dynamics involved in the original relationship. For example, a CEO might react to her chairperson as she did toward a primary school teacher from the past. If her projected emotions are negative, it can very much impact her belief in her obligations—she might perceive failure on her part or distrust from her chairperson. In contrast, if her chairperson reminds her of someone who was a positive influence, she is likely to perceive her chairperson, the organization, and her own obligations in a positive light, helping the psychological contract and, consequently, the relationship.

CORPORATE GOVERNANCE THAT IS "LIVED"

Corporate governance—the organizational guidelines, principles, rules, and procedures that define a stakeholder's rights and responsibilities—forms the "what" of a given leadership role. It does not describe how the role should be performed. This leaves a gap of understanding that individuals will fill with their own assumptions and understanding around the role and the authority it contains, forming an unconscious "how" that often drives conflict. The problem is an assumption that there is a common understanding of the role that prevents people from reflecting on potential role misperception.

An 80 percent majority of leaders interviewed stressed the importance of corporate governance's impact on relationships; they were conscious of the importance of having clear roles. However, they also said that corporate governance needed to be "lived" to be truly understood. In saying this, they were unwittingly referring to the "how" of their roles.

Some leaders stated that corporate governance had no influence on their relationships because they had a clear understanding of the role's rules and believed those rules to be aligned with both their own and their counterpart's understanding of the roles.

In most cases, unsurprisingly, this way of thinking resulted in continued conflicts within the co-leader relationship. Two leaders could be in conflict, point to the same corporate governance, and be talking about completely different things because the "how" wasn't addressed. Both parties believed they were interpreting the roles and the relationship under rational, conscious drivers, when in fact, their behavior was being driven by each person's irrational, unconscious interpretation.

For example, a CEO named Joseph attributed his conflict-ridden relationship with his chairman, Matt, to a penchant for playing politics. He said that both their roles were clearly laid out and that they were both familiar with the guidelines around them, such as the function rules and the organizational regulations; Matt just didn't seem willing to trust Joseph or let him do his job. However, when asked if they actually discussed these guidelines in detail, Joseph said they never had.

Compare that situation with Eric and Armand, chairperson and CEO respectively, who also claimed to have a clear understanding of their individual roles and the guidelines around them. Unlike Joseph and Matt's, their relationship worked very well. When asked if they had discussed their roles, they said, "Oh, yes, in detail and at length. It was hard in the beginning, but it was worth it. It is the only way to build trust and reduce misunderstandings."

If corporate governance is not "lived," it serves as a justifier of the conflict. It provides an excuse not to further analyze details or uncomfortable matters if things do not go well. On the opposite end, if roles are discussed in-depth and mutually understood, there is a chance for a healthy psychological contract. It sounds simple, but it makes a major difference in the health of a co-leader relationship.

POWER BALANCE/IMBALANCE

Throughout the interview process, leaders consistently and repeatedly alluded to power dynamics within their co-leader relationship. These allusions followed a curious pattern. Individuals were rather dismissive when asked directly about their personal understanding of power, asserting that it was not that important to them, that they didn't believe in pursuing power for its own sake. Later, however, some would make indirect statements that contradicted their original claims, such as "I do not like to play number two," "I still like to be in charge and have my say," "Power is nice—it boosts the ego," or "I enjoy the glory of being successful." Within minutes of answering questions, they unconsciously contradicted themselves about the importance of how they viewed power. It was as if they had a combined fascination for and aversion to it.

It appears that power is, more often than not, a big underlying issue in business relationships. Most leaders attributed failed relationships with their counterparts to "politics" or "strong personalities." When asked to explain these causes further, they used phrases such as "power games" and "power vacuum." While they were conscious of power as an element in the relationship, it was an unconscious driver because they were not aware of how these power struggles played into their side of the psychological contract. One major aspect of this was how it prevented them from achieving role clarity.

Demanding role clarity is, in a sense, like requesting the proper balance of power so that the other leader does not interfere. It is an important part of the psychological contract in helping maintain and achieve power bonds. The clearer the contract, the better the relationship. Relationships that lack role clarity are forced to rely on persistent power games, which negatively influence job satisfaction, performance, commitment, and retention, and ultimately lead to psychological contract breach.

TIME SPENT TOGETHER

Time is often a structural hurdle in the CEO/chairperson relationship. Unlike the CEO, the chairperson is often a part-time employee, which naturally reduces the amount of time the two spend working together.

This discrepancy of time may play out in one of three ways.

1. The CEO and chairperson want to spend time together.

Phil, a chairperson, spoke in his interview about how he and his CEO, Rob, would regularly go out for a drink and dinner together because they recognized it was crucial for their ability to build trust. Even though their paths crossed infrequently at work, they made time to meet in person or speak on the phone so that they were able to build a relationship that allowed them to cooperate productively.

2. The CEO and chairperson do not want to spend time together.

Lindsay, a chairperson, had a strained relationship with her CEO. When asked how much time they spent together, she said, "Why would I want to spend one more minute than I have to with that narcissist?" She admitted that she took the antipathy one step further, booking meetings with her CEO only to cancel half an hour before, just to demonstrate her authority, which, in her eyes, he constantly undermined. This, obviously, is a worst-case scenario—in a breakdown of the co-leader relationship like this one, people often cling to their perceived positions of power even more tightly, creating unhealthy interactions that make for an ever more toxic workplace. Generally speaking, the only way to remedy these situations is for one party to step down or, more likely, be ejected.

3. Only one party wants to spend more time together.

Willy, a chairperson, tried repeatedly to sit down and talk with Morgan, his CEO. However, Morgan resisted these attempts to spend time together. He perceived that Willy only initiated these meetings in moments of perceived crisis. Morgan felt it was better to keep Willy at a distance because he wouldn't understand the intricacies of the business. This distance communicated to Willy a lack of respect. He felt that he was not being taken seriously. While their relationship was not fraught, it was reduced to being merely transactional. They could work together in the attempt to solve a crisis, but this didn't make for productive cooperation.

However it comes about, spending less time together reduces co-leaders' communication as well as their clarity about details of their roles and relationships, leading to fewer and more ambiguous promises that can lead to incongruence. Incongruence is a critical aspect in the perception of broken promises and can harm a relationship. In general, similar to reduced trust, reduced time spent together frequently leads to inferior quality and quantity of communication and cooperation.

CASE STUDIES

Despite the unique circumstances surrounding each interviewee, their memories and experiences revealed how a combination of these unconscious drivers—family upbringing, transference, "lived" corporate governance, power balance/imbalance, and time spent—combine to greatly impact their relationships with their co-leaders and their professional satisfaction as a whole.

NEGATIVE EXAMPLE: SARA

Sara is a CEO who, during her interview, acknowledged that she had a compulsive tendency to please others—being loved by her colleagues was very important to her. Her chairperson, Jessica, played manipulatively on this value by alternating her responses to Sara's efforts to please. At times, Jessica would respond with praise and love, and at other times with punishment. Sara came to see that this was the reason she had a hard time building trust with her chairperson. Working her hardest never felt like enough. She felt insecure, lost, hurt, and exhausted.

After spending some time digging into her past memories and experiences, Sara revealed that Jessica reminded her of one of her primary school teachers. This teacher had always suppressed her, telling her that her work wasn't good enough, that she wasn't trying hard enough. As a child, this created a deep need for appreciation, especially from an authority figure; as an adult, Sara unconsciously reacted against this need by both pleasing and fighting her current authority figure—her chairperson. The relationship brought out the same insecurities she had experienced in school.

POSITIVE EXAMPLE: BRIAN

Brian, a CEO, shared that despite his confidence within his position, he always became nervous when he went to meet with his chairperson, Charles. Fearing not coming off as his best, he was hesitant about speaking his mind or being decisive in their conversations. After going through the interview process, Brian realized that Charles reminded him of his grandfather. Not only were their manners similar, but they even looked alike, wearing the same beard and round glasses. A highly critical person, Brian's grandfather always gave him the feeling that he wasn't good enough. As Brian didn't feel comfortable in Charles's presence, he reduced the time they spent together to a minimum.

By bringing this unconscious driver to his awareness, Brian was able to overcome his unproductive behavioral patterns with his chairperson. He began to see Charles for who he was, not the projection of his grandfather. For his part, Charles had no negative outlook regarding Brian's way of behaving. When Brian began to speak his mind more clearly, it actually helped their relationship. As he turned into a better leader, Brian and Charles were able to be a better team. Brian started to enjoy the productive time he had with Charles.

TAPPING THE UNCONSCIOUS

Almost all the interviewees knew hardly anything about what made up their counterpart's personality. They knew about their education, track record, and marital status, but next to nothing about their upbringings, such as whether they had siblings, or any of their formative experiences. If you find yourself asking why your co-leader relationship is not working, despite the work you've put in to fix it, it is time to look beyond the conscious. You need to find out what unconsciously affects you and your co-leader, and what might be intensifying these drivers of conflict.

Chief among these intensifiers is birth order. It is no accident that top-level executives are frequently firstborn children in their family, or else they played a traditional "firstborn" role. Parenting expert Michael Grose, the author of the book *Why First Borns Rule the World and Last Borns Want to Change It*, says, "The family provides the frame for the children's development, and birth order provides the lens through which each child sees the world individually."[5] For firstborn children, this lens typically includes a lesser degree of trust, as well as an instinct to compete with others for attention and appreciation. Combine two firstborns in a co-leader relationship, and it will likely explain why so many of these relationships result in conflict.

Along with birth order, lack of self-awareness is a critical intensifier of how conflict is magnified in their experience. Although there will always be unconscious drivers at work in their behavior, becoming more self-aware can bring these drivers to the conscious mind, helping people take responsibility for, and exert authority over, the experiences in their lives.

In the next section, we will closely examine how conscious and unconscious drivers and intensifiers work together to shape executive relationships.

PART II

——

THE INTENSIFIERS
OF CONFLICT

CHAPTER 4

BIRTH ORDER

During my research, most of my interviews of leaders began with simple questions about where they grew up and whether they had siblings. I quickly discovered that even these innocuous questions were uncomfortable for most interviewees to address. Top leaders seem to prefer not to think and even less to talk about how their childhood experiences might impact their professional identities and destiny. They could talk about business all day, but a common reaction to questions touching on their childhood was to cross their arms and turn quiet.

Still, the more they shared about their childhoods, the more obvious it became that some of their behavior patterns in co-leader relationships stemmed from experiences in those formative years. After the fifth or sixth interview, a new and significant finding emerged related to birth order. I was surprised to discover that 95 percent of my interviewees were "functional firstborns." I started to adjust my questions around what role they played in their family as children and what role they find themselves playing in their own families today. People tend to act, even later in life, according to the role they played within their family during childhood. Questions about their role in their family led the interviewees to reveal that their upbringing marked them very strongly. Many added that they never reflected on their upbringing or shared it with anyone; however, once they started talking about it, it was hard for them to stop. It seemed they found the experience enjoyable and liberating.

With each additional interview, it became obvious that birth order had a more significant bearing on leaders' behavior than I had first imagined. Almost all the individuals I interviewed were either biological firstborns or so-called functional firstborns (FFBs). The patterns here were anything but random—firstborn children and FFBs shared a set of characteristics that created a clear pathway to their behavior as leaders.

Before we go into those characteristics and how they shape executive behavior, it is important to understand what a functional firstborn might look like.

EXAMPLES OF THE FUNCTIONAL FIRSTBORN

Tim, a chairperson, was not a biological firstborn. In fact, he was a middle child—number three out of six. But when asked about his role in the family, he said it was "a weird one," and described himself as having been "the source of hope" in his family. As the first boy, he was moved into the role of firstborn. His parents held him up to his siblings as a model of behavior; he was pushed to excel in school; he felt it was his duty to be the peacekeeper in the house. He became comfortable with being in charge and shouldering the pressure and responsibility that came with that. His siblings accepted him in this role; even later in life, they asked him to speak at their weddings and at their parents' funerals. A major part of this functional firstborn role was Tim's relationship to his father. His father's constant praise and consistent pushing made him feel that he needed to be highly regarded in his father's eyes.

When it came to his co-leader relationship at work, Tim talked about how important power was to his CEO. This might very well have been the case. On the other hand, his upbringing shaped him as well. He realized that he was accustomed to assuming full responsibility and leadership and being "the source of hope," and felt challenged by the mere presence of another authority figure.

Mary, also a chairperson, was the second-born in her

family, with a brother eighteen months older than she. Since girls generally develop more quickly at young ages than boys, it is not unusual for girls born closely after a boy to assume a second firstborn role or even take over the firstborn role. Furthermore, since Mary's brother was not close to their father, she replaced him as the successor to the family business. While her parents never explicitly placed pressure on her, she grew up feeling the weight of obligation of fulfilling the caretaking and peacemaking role in the family. Like Tim, she said that her parents put all their hope in her, and that her family still does today.

DEFINING THE FUNCTIONAL FIRSTBORN

Both the above cases illustrate that the firstborn role is defined less by the numerical birth order and more by the perceived relationship between a child and their parents and their siblings. It simply happens that biological first-borns are typically the beneficiaries of the competition for parental attention by virtue of having more time to form that relationship. According to Dr. Kevin Leman, psychologist and author of numerous books on families and birth order, firstborns receive up to 3,000 more hours of quality time with their parents between the ages of four and thirteen.

Yet, as seen with Tim and Mary, that relationship does not have to be biologically based. In some cases, functional firstborns might even be the youngest in their family. This happens most often when there is an age gap of at least five years between them and their next older sibling, or if they are the first boy or girl in a family. In large families, two or more groups of siblings can emerge, allowing for more than one firstborn role to exist.

"Only children" who have no siblings are also known as super firstborns. They are included in the FFB category because they are both privileged and burdened with receiving all parental expectations and resources. They show the same characteristics as firstborns and FFBs, but often in more extreme forms (e.g., ultra-perfectionists). They tend to act unusually mature for their age, coming across as adults at the age of seven or eight. Having never been forced to compete for attention, they often become more self-centered and less inclined toward instinctive reciprocity. During my interviews with leaders, this was demonstrated by the tendency of only children/ super firstborns to be less talkative—more prodding was required to get information out of them. In addition, they generally are quite independent—often, they do not understand why siblings fight amongst themselves.

CHARACTERISTICS OF FIRSTBORNS

Today's leaders who were only children come from a time when families were larger on average, which means there are relatively fewer of them. However, with the trend of family sizes getting smaller in the Western world, there will be more single-child households. In the future, more super firstborns will most likely become similar to regular firstborns.

Many studies over the years have revealed that one of the standout characteristics of firstborns and FFBs is their tendency to exhibit higher IQs than later-borns. They generally are also consistently more determined, responsible, reliable, and academically successful. For this reason, they tend to be natural leaders. They grow up being goal-oriented, organized, and ambitious, as well as critical and overly sensitive about errors. Perfectionism is a common trait, and they are more likely to suffer from burnout or a midlife crisis. Because parents are generally stricter with firstborns than with their later-born children, they tend to have more pressure on them to follow the rules. As a result, ideas of authority are likely to become quite important to them.

Firstborns also tend to be analytical and skeptical, less trusting, and less prone to respond reciprocally than later-borns. This combination of traits, along with the fear of dethronement occasioned by the arrival of siblings, breeds a tendency toward anxiety along with its physical manifestations, such as migraines, and stomach and back pains.

In 2011, a Gallup study based in New Mexico revealed that if Americans could only have one child, they preferred a boy 40 percent of the time and a girl 28 percent of the time, with the remaining 22 percent having no preference. This is almost identical to statistics measured in 1941, which showed Americans preferring boys 38 percent of the time and girls 24 percent. Men skewed the results because 49 percent preferred boys, while only 22 percent preferred girls. Women's preference for a boy was at 31 percent and for a girl at 33 percent. Furthermore, preference for a boy baby was inversely related to age. Those younger than thirty years old chose a boy 54 percent of the time and a girl 27 percent. The margins decreased for those aged thirty to forty-nine and again for those aged fifty to sixty-four. The highest preference for boys was amongst men under fifty, while women under fifty broke even in their preference, and those over fifty preferred a girl.

Americans with lower education levels were also more likely to prefer a boy, while those people with post-graduate education broke even in preferences. Higher or lower income had no bearing on preferences. In 2017, a new study was conducted that revealed a decrease in the margins of preference, but boys were still favored.

In East Asia and Eastern Europe, there are 117 million women believed to be missing as a consequence of son preference and gender-based sex selection. In India, there are 110 boys for every 100 girls, while in China, it is almost 116 boys for 100 girls. The trend continues in places like Georgia, Azerbaijan, Armenia, Albania, Singapore, and Vietnam and speaks to the characteristics imposed on firstborns.

Their tendency to strive for power later in life is easy to link with an attempt to reclaim power lost in childhood. It was found that firstborn status more accurately predicted cooperativeness than age, sex, income, or even religion. In general, firstborns have a clear sense of right and wrong and are quite rigid with its interpretation.

Their communication style tends to be more dominant and instructive, rather than collaborative. Thus, two first-borns working together often find themselves locked in power struggles, both fighting for dominance and neither willing to make compromises.

Most behaviors and characteristics that children exhibit are thought to stem from the amount of parents' attention. Concerning firstborns, parents tend to over-respond to their actions and behaviors with praise, in addition to pushing too hard for performance. Everything the child does is a big deal.

Unlike second- and third-borns, who have another child to measure themselves against, firstborns have no reference point, forcing them to be self-referential. This has a significant effect on how they try to achieve goals throughout their lives. While later-born children are more likely to be oriented toward outperforming others, firstborns are oriented toward mastery, always aiming to improve their own performance.

As the saying goes, firstborns are the "guinea pigs." Their upbringing is subject to the anxiety of first-time parents who are still figuring out how to rear a child. The firstborn is commonly overprotected, as well as subject to stricter rules and discipline to make up for common inconsistency in parenting. Because firstborns learn primarily from their parents as their main point of reference, they end up idolizing them as perfect people, internalizing the sometimes too-high standards set for them. Despite often feeling that they cannot meet their parents' expectations, they grow up unconsciously determined to live up to them.

HISTORY OF BIRTH ORDER RESEARCH

The discussions surrounding the long-term impacts of a person's position among siblings date back to 1874. These began when explorer, anthropologist, and geneticist Sir Francis Galton reported that eldest sons were overrepresented as members of the Royal Society. Later, Austrian behavioral psychologist Dr. Alfred Adler formulated a theory that it wasn't the numerical birth order alone that functioned as a personality determinant, but it was equally about the psychological birth order. His theory emphasized the situation a child was born into and the way the child interpreted it. This theory opened the door for more research around the world. Soon, it became a widely accepted idea that personality was strongly influenced by birth order.

In 1996, psychologist and MIT history of science specialist Dr. Frank J. Sulloway wrote an extensive work called *Born to Rebel* that compiled twenty-six years of experience concerning birth order. It gained wide exposure and was well supported by scientific research. This book, along-side the many best-selling books of Kevin Leman, have become some of the most widely read and referenced research to date on birth order and psychological birth order. Their work and others' proved to be seminal not only to interpreting my interviews with CEOs and chair-persons, but also to understanding my own experience that started it all.

MY CEO AND ME

My former CEO once told me he was born in week twenty-four of his mother's pregnancy. Having begun his life fighting for survival, this became his way of being in the world, as he stated. A painful professional setback early in his career seems to have driven him harder in trying to avoid failure. As I mentioned in the Introduction, despite the fact that the reasons behind his separation from the company were never told to the press, a news-paper published an article stating that he was fired for poor performance. Some could speculate that this must have reopened some childhood wounds for him; his retal-iatory campaign to build a rival business and poach our employees looked very much like a contest of survival, in keeping with his life motto.

He does not seem to be alone in this "fight for survival" mindset. Both the former and current president of FIFA had a similar experience of being born much too early and fighting for survival. This childhood trauma most likely seeped into their understanding of the world, leading them to adopt and cultivate a strong personality and a distinct attitude toward the importance of being in power.

Examining the upbringing of individuals like these also revealed that it is very likely that the way they came to handle power relates to how they were treated by their primary caregivers. For one thing, parents who fight for their child's survival often communicate indirectly that the world is not a safe place.

Psychologist and psychoanalyst Erik Erikson developed a theory of eight stages of psychosocial development that is considered a milestone in explaining human development. His theory elucidates the link between an individual's predispositions and their environment.

In infancy (zero to eighteen months), Erikson's first stage, a child looks for stability, consistency, and comfort to meet its basic needs. Severe incidents that take place at or right after birth (such as a premature birth that threatens the child's survival) prevent the child from developing a foundation of affection, security, and stability that allows them to trust the world and even themselves.

Erikson's second stage (eighteen months to three years) is

concerned with autonomy versus shame and self-doubt. In attempting to answer the question "Is it OK to be me?" the child looks for clues in how its caregivers allow it to explore, experiment, and even ask for assistance as it seeks to assert its will. A lack of self-esteem in this stage, caused by too much control or criticism, can trigger doubt, shame, and lack of self-consciousness. In response, the child may develop too much pride as an instinctive method of defense. Such children are very likely to develop a sense of mistrust, which leads to insecurity, anxiety, and frustration, driving them to seek out stability in the form of power. In addition, it is reasonable to assume that these parents have a tendency to overprotect and overpamper them. Growing up under this circumstance, the child craves special treatment as a necessity; losing it makes them fearful for their own survival.

While individual leaders with this personality may flourish, issues usually arise when they are confronted with someone whose leadership style is equally strong. When those two styles are in conflict, they can harm a company. This is how my situation with my CEO devolved.

Like my CEO, I too was an FFB. I grew up with an older brother who experienced severe bullying during his childhood. He was the "perfect victim": kind, helpful, very good at school, and a bit shy. When I was just five or six years old, my parents gave me the task of walking with him to school in hopes that the two of us together would discourage older children from bullying him. This small action helped me develop a sense of caretaking and empowerment that I carry with me today; my instinct is to help others enable their potential. Needless to say, my worldview sharply conflicted with my CEO's Darwinist "survival of the fittest" mentality. His nature to fight opposed my nature to defend, and this opposition negatively shaped how we interacted with each other. At the same time, my caretaking instinct led me to give him the benefit of the doubt for far too long.

While on one hand, my CEO and I demonstrated similar birth order rank characteristics, on the other hand, we developed almost opposite worldviews. These aspects did not combine well in creating a high-functioning relationship.

FFBS IN THE UPPER RANKS

In 2012, psychology professors Dr. Daniel Eckstein and Dr. Jason A. Kauffman published a study that revealed how overwhelmingly overrepresented firstborns are in management. Functional firstborns prove to be the most likely to inhabit higher-ranking positions not only in business, but also in science, medicine, engineering, journalism, and politics. They are the students and professors at universities and business schools, US presidents, prime ministers, women with doctorates, and Nobel Prize winners, and comprise the majority of the US's who's who lists. This trend is so prevalent that in some high-level international business networks, firstborns account for more than 90 percent of the members.

How do these mind-blowing statistics come about? Some researchers point to the abundance of resources and quality time firstborns receive from their parents. Firstborn children are naturally groomed to expect, ask for, and receive the resources that build up their sense of personal power. Furthermore, other studies claim that family order naturally trains firstborns in leadership skills, as they are often tasked with managing their younger siblings and setting a good example for them. Other researchers also point to the higher IQs of firstborns as well as their need for perfection and pleasing others.

In other words, there is no single factor that makes firstborns more likely to assume positions of leadership and power. Rather, it is the combination of many different factors that determines the path and personality of firstborn children, along with the forces that help determine personality in later-born children.

WHAT ABOUT THE NON-FFBS?

Of all children in the birth order, middle-borns usually

have the hardest role to define. With the "source of hope" position already occupied by the firstborn, middle children often try to differentiate themselves by finding their own niche. Very often, this leads them to adopt characteristics that are the opposite of the child above them, which also holds true for second-borns, who can be middle-borns or last-borns. Middle-borns may take the path of being determined nonconformists, or they might develop the characteristics of another child whom they spend a lot of time around, whether it be another sibling or a friend.

Research reveals middle-born children to be socially skilled, loyal, and oriented toward prioritizing friendship. They display less anxiety and fear and tend to be good mediators and negotiators. They dislike conflict, making them more likely to be diplomatic and seek compromise. Because they are not pushed as hard as firstborns and are not expected to accomplish as much, they have no qualms about being occasionally laid-back, and they tend to get away with it. Career-wise, middle-born children tend to be trial lawyers (capitalizing on their mediation and compromise skills), entrepreneurs (making use of their determination to be different), mediators, social workers, or activists (perhaps to compensate for the injustice many of them experienced as children).

Youngest children are inveterate attention seekers, quickly becoming the little stars of the family—the ones who get away with everything. Used to being picked on by their older siblings, they learn to entertain others and deflect negativity at an early age. As they grow up, they tend to be very social, outgoing, spontaneous, and humorous. They are often class clowns, charismatic, and unlikely to get punished for their escapades. They are usually drawn to careers as actors, talk show hosts, comedians, psychologists, and salespeople.

No matter what precise order they fall in, later-borns are generally more carefree and gregarious, and they enjoy surprises. As a result, they are open to new experiences and tend to like change. When it comes to jobs, they gravitate toward occupations on the basis of contributing to humankind and making the world a better place. They take more risks and are more willing than firstborns to endorse innovation, favor radical perspectives, and embrace challenges to conventional ways of thinking.

It must be noted that all of these qualities exhibited by later-borns are just as essential to an organization as the qualities of firstborns. There are exceptions to these roles, but in general, organizations tend to operate very much according to these family dynamics. If a mediator or negotiator position is needed, a middle-born may be the most suitable for that role, while later-borns might be better suited as change agents and transformers. For this reason, diversity in an organization is also a must. It expands the scope of the roles being filled and provides an opportunity for people to better communicate.

Although most people in top leadership positions are functional firstborns, new organizational models, such as boundaryless companies, call for new leadership styles. People with different birth ranks may be better suited to fill these roles. It will be interesting to see whether the overrepresentation of firstborns within leadership roles is reduced as a result.

THE BIGGER PICTURE

Birth order is not the sole determinant of someone's fate in an organization; rather, it is an intensifier of the conscious and unconscious drivers within their perspective and personality. Knowing that firstborns, in general, are more likely to run into power and dominance struggles with other firstborns—that their issues with authority may stem from a fear of dethronement or a determination to protect someone as if they were a younger sibling—contributes to understanding conflict at its psychological root.

The important takeaway is that understanding birth order and the ways in which it might factor into your psychological drivers enables you to use your own traits and characteristics to your advantage.

The understanding of birth order is not a hard science—for example, it cannot be measured with any types of formulas or in a laboratory. As with many aspects of life that do not perfectly fit into a mold, birth order does not consistently fit into neat statistical databases.

Birth order rank, behavior, and personality traits are not inherently good or bad; they are simply different from one another. Without them, we would all be little different from robots. The key is understanding how they shape a professional environment.

Kevin Leman writes, "If you realize what's in your background, evaluate how you responded to it then and how you respond to it now, and decide you want to move on from here, then you can get somewhere."[6] Analyzing the way your birth order impacted you is not about blaming parents. They did the best that they could while operating according to their own unconscious patterns and values. Rather, the value lies in absorbing the thought and research on birth order and examining how it accounts for conflict, power dynamics, trust, goals, and transference. Being aware of these forces will only work to your advantage. The more you learn about yourself and your employees, the more likely you are to cater to them to contribute to their happiness. This will naturally lead to increased productivity, loyalty, and creativity.

CHAPTER 5

LACK OF SELF-AWARENESS

Steve's employees knew him as a sarcastic CEO. His penchant for needling people, making cutting remarks, and sometimes outright attacking others made people afraid of him, preventing anyone from alerting him to the toxic effect of his behavior. Furthermore, because no one dared show weakness in his presence for fear of being ridiculed or attacked, the productivity of the company suffered.

For his part, Steve had no idea how strong the effect of his sarcasm was. It was a habit he developed from growing up in a big family with a lot of competition among his siblings; harsh communications paired with a thick-skinned insensitivity to others were his methods of defense—his way to survive.

It took a coach for Steve to become aware of his negative behavior patterns and what triggered these responses in him. As long as he didn't know what was going on, he couldn't take responsibility for his actions and his behavior. He could only change when he brought these behaviors from the unconscious to the conscious. He then saw how strongly they influenced his worldview and the way he affected others.

WHAT DOES SELF-AWARENESS REALLY MEAN?

People like Steve are criticized or labeled because nobody knows anything about their life or upbringing. Often, they do not even know how their own experiences have affected them. They have no way to change their behavior until they develop self-awareness.

Self-awareness means deeply understanding one's own emotions, strengths, and limitations. It involves recognizing one's values and motives, and thinking things over rather than acting impulsively based on emotion.

This isn't to say emotion should be ignored—far from it, in fact. Dr. Daniel Goleman, a psychologist and author of numerous books, such as *Emotional Intelligence*, that popularized the concept of emotional intelligence, says that self-awareness starts with paying attention to feelings and the way they shape perceptions, thoughts, and actions. It is a tool that helps manage complex situations, both personal and professional.

Developing self-awareness does not happen overnight—it takes time to step back and self-reflect. This is one reason why so few leaders have a high level of self-awareness until an impending crisis pushes them to think deeply about themselves. For some, agreeing to be interviewed for this book proved to be a catalyst for becoming more self-aware.

SELF-AWARENESS IN THE EXECUTIVE LEADER

Once you learn about the drivers of conflict (such as upbringing) as well as how the past shapes you, it becomes easier to look at your co-leader relationship objectively. You can begin to put yourself in the other person's shoes more often rather than taking a defensive posture. You can take measures to strengthen your sensitivities and overcome reactionary responses.

For example, if you become aware that you are sensitive to criticism and understand what influences or experiences from your past have made you that way, you can reframe how you hear your co-leader's negative comments in a way that makes them feel less personal. Or if the converse is true—that you find your co-leader reacting defensively to your comments—you can examine your behavior (like Steve did), looking for possible drivers that may be influencing your language or tone and use that knowledge to improve the way you communicate.

The first step is to bring a pattern of behavior or response into your consciousness and decide whether it is productive for you. The second step is to learn from the past about where that behavior comes from, rewrite the script of your "inner theater" around that behavior, and use this new script to change your actions.

This thoughtful approach to human interaction is critical. The key is self-leadership: the ability to consciously influence your thoughts and behaviors in the process of achieving your personal and professional goals. Human beings tend to act on impulse. When presented with a challenge, they are prone to fight back, seek revenge, or simply ignore and disconnect or give up. If you can learn which negative conflict-ridden behaviors you are prone to, you can grab them the moment they show up, sit with them for a moment, and make an empowered decision whether to react the way you always have or go down another, more productive road. It takes practice, but it is ultimately choosing to simplify a situation that conflict would only make more complicated.

Shedding light on your so-called darker sides can be an uncomfortable experience. But doing so will help you develop as a person and as a leader. It will also empower you to shape your situation rather than let circumstances and other people dictate your future. By making the conscious decision to break unproductive patterns in your behavior, you are better able to use your energy, focus, and creativity.

As mentioned earlier, the first step toward psychological well-being is psychological awareness. You cannot wait around and expect the people around you and your environment to change. The responsibility is on you to make the change and cultivate your own psychological awareness. (We will discuss this in greater depth in Part Three.)

HOW AWARE ARE WE?

As I conducted interviews with different leaders, it became apparent that some people were already more self-reflective and self-aware than others. It was less about the statements they made, such as "I am aware of my patterns" or "A leader has to understand him- or herself to understand others," than it was about their experience with coaching or time spent in personal reflection.

You might assume that leaders who had gone through particularly life-altering experiences—severe illnesses, significant personal losses, long-lasting family issues over family business succession, blended families resulting in a new arrangement of birth order rank—would be more apt to acknowledge how those experiences had shaped them. However, among those leaders with life-changing experiences, some were highly self-aware while others were not. The differentiating factor was primarily having actively done the work of personal reflection. Without exception, those who had gone through therapy or coaching, for instance, didn't back away from talking about their childhood during interviews. On the contrary, they were quite comfortable talking about their upbringing and how experiences had impacted them. They were also consistent in their responses, where others would in many cases contradict themselves (especially when it came to discussing the importance of power or public image).

Reflection is less rational than thinking. Personality coaching enhances reflection, which leads to increased self-awareness. Even Bob Nardelli, the former CEO of The Home Depot, Inc., is quoted as saying, "I absolutely believe that people, unless coached, never reach their maximum capabilities."[7]

YOU CANNOT HELP OTHERS IF YOU CANNOT HELP YOURSELF

Becoming more self-aware has the additional benefit of helping you understand your co-leader. While self-awareness starts with recognizing what's going on with you, it culminates in recognizing what's going on with other people.

When talking to CEOs and chairpersons about their conflicts with their counterparts, I found that often they didn't know much, if anything, about the person sitting across from them at the board table. They knew very little about the other person's family or where they were from—just the basic facts related to education, track record, and perhaps (though not always) their marital status. This was the case in both leaders who showed self-awareness and those who did not.

While it can help with understanding others, one-sided awareness in a relationship does not seem to be sufficient. This seemed especially true if people had the perception that their counterparts were not self-aware at all. However, if both co-leaders developed self-awareness and believed that the other party did so, too, each side felt empowered to respond productively instead of reacting to drivers, and the relationship functioned much better.

EPIPHANY ISN'T ENOUGH

Breaking instinctive habits and behaviors is not easy. Smokers who consciously want to give up smoking are a good example. Despite being very aware of how much they want to change, the strength of their habit makes quitting exceptionally difficult.

Even people who are fully invested in changing their behavior let hidden competing commitments unconsciously undermine their big commitments (something we will cover in greater detail later in the book). A crisis created by ongoing conflict may lead to an epiphany, but as valuable as an epiphany is to bring unconscious elements into consciousness, it isn't enough on its own. Sustainable change is most likely to occur through making small, incremental choices and taking actions that pave the way to the desired new behavior. Like working out and building muscle, it is a process.

Ronnie was a CEO who grew up in a wealthy background until her father lost everything. In one fell swoop, a failed venture swept away all the family's assets, even their home, and left them very poor. This experience shaped Ronnie; as a consequence, she became highly risk-averse. She could not make a decision without having first collected all the information available about it. Her subconscious instincts had formed around never again being caught unaware. Nobody around her knew about the past experience influencing her behavior or even thought to look behind the scenes at what could be causing it—they just privately wondered how a CEO could be so risk-averse.

Simply remembering and confronting this seminal experience wouldn't be enough to change Ronnie's behavior in a sustainable way. Although this first step is important, she would have to take the further step of rewriting the script of her inner theater. To put it another way, she would have to consciously rewire the unconscious drivers of her behavior. Starting with the acknowledgment that she was no longer in danger of losing everything, she could acknowledge her restrictive tendency, consciously choose to take the risks necessary for a successful CEO, and see the resulting improvement in her company's morale and performance.

The mental world is a complex thing. It is crucial to identify cognitive processes and distortions to understand how unconscious behaviors such as transference, or intensifiers such as birth order, interfere with your leadership style, actions, and processes. Once you are more aware of these, you can begin seeing how the various drivers and intensifiers work in concert with each other—for better or for worse. Understanding their interaction will have a huge impact on your psychological contracts, on relationships, and ultimately, on what you really want for your organization.

CHAPTER 6

TOXIC COMBINATIONS

Between 2008 and 2013 alone, Switzerland saw several cases in which well-known and successful leaders took their own lives, such as the CEOs of Julius Baer, Swisscom, Ricola, and Zurich Insurance Group, as well as the last company's CFO.

In many of these cases, the motivations are unknown. In others, however, the available information offers the opportunity for important insights into why someone in this lofty position might have ended their life in such a tragic manner.

Such is the case with Swisscom CEO Carsten Schloter. Carsten grew up as the middle child between three sisters. In interviews, he stated that he had great difficulties in his childhood accepting authority, a tendency that indicates that as the only son in the family, he felt pressure put on him. Having assumed the role of a functional firstborn, it appears that he was motivated by a desire for a sense of having everything under control, bearing responsibilities for others, and achieving perfection.

Carsten spent his career working toward the point when he would be in a position he believed would make him safe. The achievement of this trajectory came with being hired as CEO of Swisscom, a major telecommunications provider in Switzerland. But most likely, his sense of security changed when the company brought in a new chairperson. It appears that the shift in the power balance created new pressures on Carsten that he became less and less able to cope with.

Throughout his career, Carsten's style was known to be always on, full-force forward. In a newspaper interview, he was quoted as saying, "I notice that I find it increasingly difficult to calm down and to reduce tempo."[8] In another interview, he confessed that modern means of communication have their bad sides, too, the most dangerous of which is finding oneself in a state of permanent activity. He admitted that he found himself constantly checking his smartphone for messages and emails; he said it was impossible to find rest and reduce the pace.

Apparently, he also found it very difficult to seek out help or support. Certain employees reported later that he had mentioned having severe sleep issues. However, when they asked if he still had everything under control, he said that of course he did. This attitude also got the better of him in his personal life. He was separated from his wife of many years, having left her and their three young children for a younger employee at work. Between the painful flux of his private life and the restructuring of the business under the new leadership dynamic, Carsten suffered from the sense that he was losing control of almost every aspect of his life. Supposedly, his only method of coping with the growing pressure was to work even harder despite knowing at some level that this was causing him to suffer even more. In a May 2013 interview, just two months before he died, Carsten identified himself as a "driven man" and was quoted as saying, "I always have the feeling that I only run from commitment to commitment. It makes you feel as if you are being strangled."[9]

It looks as though the combination of his upbringing as a functional firstborn, not being able to shut off, and feeling that he had failed as a father and husband ended up being a toxic combination Carsten couldn't figure out how to handle—he was only forty-nine years old when he took his life. At his funeral, his older sister was quoted as saying, "As always, you undertook your last decision by yourself. But in contrast to what you always believed, you actually were never alone."[10]

Shortly after Carsten's suicide there followed the case of Martin Senn, who served as CEO of Zurich Insurance Group for six years before being laid off at fifty-nine years old. Like Carsten, he was also the only boy in his family, born between two older sisters and a younger sister. When he was a teenager, his younger sister died in an accident. Shortly afterward, his father died. Before their deaths, Martin was always a bad scholar, but that quickly took a 180-degree turn in the wake of these significant losses. He became best in his class. At age fourteen, Martin assumed the father role in his family and turned his whole life around so that he could take care of his mother and his sisters.

Martin grew up to be a highly successful CEO. His career was untainted by any failures, scandals, or major losses. Personality-wise, he was reported to be very modest and, as a result, was put under pressure by investors to be more aggressive. At one point, profits fell by 53 percent, forcing him to cancel 8,000 jobs worldwide. This setback marked his perception of himself; for perhaps the first time ever, he felt like a failure, especially once the company chairperson laid him off and assumed the role of interim CEO. A year afterward, in 2016, Martin committed suicide.

Companions of Martin acknowledged that he defined himself by his job and had difficulty separating himself from his work identity. His reactions seem to have been tethered to his past. It can be assumed that stepping into the father role had shaped his life strategy, making him feel that he wasn't allowed to fail.

PRESSURE AND PERSPECTIVES

In both the cases of Carsten and Martin, birth order, relationship to power, and role clarity all played a part in the tragedies that followed from a perceived failure. For each of them, their decline started with a perceived early childhood crisis that was reactivated by circumstances much later in life. Both keenly felt the pressure from changes in their company environment. Both felt they couldn't show any signs of weakness. Like most CEOs, they had no one to talk with about the pain and pressure they were suffering; because of this, their emotions hit a critical point. Carsten's drive for perfection seems to have led to a constant state of anxiety where he couldn't relax, step back, and balance his work life with his personal life. Because of his issues with authority, he found himself in a constant power struggle with his chairperson. Martin apparently didn't learn how to cope with the immense pressure put on him (by others but mainly by himself) not to fail his family after the death of his father. He didn't know how to separate his work identity from his personal identity, and the perceived failure proved too much for him.

It is important not to underestimate how deep these

patterns run. They develop unconsciously throughout a person's growth from childhood to adulthood, but if they are never brought to the person's awareness, they can compromise not only the culture, productivity, and performance of a workplace, but even an individual's life. While death and suicide are the more extreme consequences, failing to examine these drivers more often results in health issues, sleep deprivation, and the intensifying of fears, doubts, emotions, anger, and temper. Looking back, this seems to be the case with my former CEO, who seems not to have taken the opportunity afforded by his professional setbacks to examine his patterns of behavior.

TOXICITY'S TOLL

There is no exact science to measure how deeply drivers of conflict influence people. It is usually a combination of several drivers working at once, which makes for complex territory. While it does not seem to be rocket science to examine conscious and unconscious drivers, nevertheless, many people still find this underlying dynamic challenging to talk about.

Some people just accept that as a leader in an international business, the constant presence of conflict is just the way business is. It is essential to realize that while this is indeed common, it does not *have* to be that way.

In fact, business works better when the relational environment is more fluid. Power games are unnecessary and benefit no one. Unhappy employees and unhealthy leaders focused on power gains are unproductive. In fact, unhealthy conflicts left unaddressed end up destroying company value. The cost isn't just individuals' mental health; it is also the company's bottom line. There is huge financial potential that can be tapped by fostering and working on healthy relationships.

The objective is certainly not to create a work environment so harmonious that it is completely conflict-free. That would be an illusion. In fact, a certain amount of tension is healthy, but only when trust can be built on it. The goal is to be constantly working on improving, little by little, as the following examples demonstrate.

EXAMPLE #1: LUCAS AND CARLOS

Lucas and Carlos both had the role of firstborn in their families. Lucas, the chairperson, was an only child. Carlos, the CEO, was the youngest in his family but had an age gap of eight years between himself and the next older sibling. When Carlos assumed the position of CEO, he realized that Lucas had been in the chairperson position for a very long time, which might lead people to see Lucas as the managing director and boss instead of him. In order to send a clear signal of his authority, Carlos's first action as CEO was to combine two offices into one, creating an office that was bigger than the chairperson's.

Lucas wasn't very happy with this being Carlos's first action as CEO—he saw it as a power play. To cement his power as chairperson—that is, the "real boss"—Lucas traded for a parking space closest to the building entrance, a space that used to belong to the CEO before Carlos.

The power games only continued from there. When Carlos and Lucas had their first meeting, Lucas made sure it took place in his office, so he would have home territory advantage. But upon walking into the meeting, Carlos unconsciously spread his cell phone, car keys, and documents out in front of him on the meeting table. Lucas did the same, also unconsciously, creating and defending his territory.

In a subsequent meeting, Carlos canceled with just an hour's notice due to an emergency. Lucas was upset by this, seeing it as Carlos using a flimsy excuse to show his power. In the next meeting, both took a break to use the bathroom. Lucas was the first to return, but instead of returning to the meeting room, he went to the receptionist to assign her tasks until Carlos reentered the room first. This sent a message that the CEO should wait for him, not the other way around.

This power struggle, which emerged right off the bat, ended up costing the company a lot of time and energy because neither party wanted to trust each other or make compromises.

EXAMPLE #2: ROGER AND SHEENA

Roger and Sheena, both firstborns in their families, were chairperson and CEO, respectively. In Roger's childhood home, he realized that there was constant mistrust in his family; as a result, he held trust in high regard for himself and was very sensitive to its breach. In Sheena's family, on the other hand, trust was held in very high regard, so she became equally sensitive to breach.

Despite their similar convictions about the importance of trust, both Roger and Sheena largely withheld it from each other. When asked about their relationship in an interview, both essentially said that they gave the other the benefit of the doubt. However, Roger added that in order for him to give someone the benefit of the doubt, he needed to "see proof very quickly." In other words, the trust clearly wasn't there. (Nor, for that matter, as he admitted, was self-awareness.)

Sheena felt the absence of this trust—being expected to quickly provide "proof" interfered with her ability to implement plans. She felt like she wasn't able to provide the quality and thorough planning that was typical of her; consequently, her solutions lacked creativity. She didn't understand why Roger didn't trust her more and realized she was becoming less trustful of him. She also began to wonder if he had a hidden agenda.

On Roger's end, he didn't even feel comfortable with the amount of trust he had granted his CEO. To him, it was important to see results quickly because he was worried she would misuse the room he gave her or even try to oust him from the throne by using information against him.

Because of their mutual mistrust, they both decided that they didn't want to spend any more time with the other than necessary. What little communication they did have, they made sure was in written form, in case they needed proof or protection.

EXAMPLE #3: BILL AND VLADIMIR

When Bill, the chairperson, was asked what power meant to him in his interview, he said, "I'm not interested in publicity and fame. I do not need anyone's applause." Minutes later, though, in a different context, he contradicted himself, saying that he liked getting applause and that "it was really nice to earn laurels."

Bill's CEO, Vladimir, had actually undergone extensive

coaching and was aware not only of his own strengths and weaknesses but also of Bill's ambivalence when it came to power. Recognizing that ambivalence as a lack of self-awareness on Bill's part, Vladimir developed empathy toward his chairperson and learned not to take every action too personally.

However, Vladimir felt he had a very clear understanding of his role in the company and wasn't willing to back down when it came to matters for which he was responsible. For example, when Bill took up a lot of airtime during an important press conference, Vladimir realized that his one-sided self-awareness wasn't sufficient in certain contexts of their relationship. However, he also knew that Bill wasn't very open to feedback and tended to take it as criticism. Vladimir's options were to either leave his post or encourage his chairperson to take on a coach.

While Bill knew deep down that the spotlight in that situation should have belonged to the CEO, he enjoyed occupying the stage and couldn't help soaking up the attention. He also felt that, as the boss, he couldn't let the CEO smell too much of that sweet morning air, lest he become more dominant. Here, the drivers of conflict were a one-sided lack of self-awareness, role clarity, and balance of power.

EXAMPLE #4: HIEN AND FREDDY

Hien had been with the same company for twenty years. After being CEO for eight, she assumed the position of chairperson and was now the most senior member of the board and management. As such, she took the lead in the search for a new CEO.

Freddy, her favorite candidate, came from outside the company. When Freddy started, she made sure to tell him as much as possible about her experience as the previous CEO. Sometimes she would get frustrated by how long it took him to get to know the business and make connections between past events and current risks. She wanted to make sure he stayed on track.

Freddy was very pleased with being selected to work for this prestigious company, but he knew he could bring a lot more to the table. He had extensive experience in different companies and industries, nationally and internationally, including turnarounds. He liked Hien and thought they would get along great because she knew the company so well. But when Freddy finally started work, he realized he was being micromanaged. He wanted to build trust with her but knew that it would take time. Although he knew she didn't mean to, Freddy felt Hien was still acting like the CEO, and he found it quite annoying. Even some of his management team and employees behaved differently when she was present.

He couldn't help but feel this undermined his position and credibility.

Unfortunately, the situation didn't get better with time. Freddy thought that a possible solution could be to spend less time with Hien in order to take advantage of the imbalance of information and control of the company's key resources that he could use as leverage. Inevitably, communication got worse. They both perceived breaches of their initial psychological contract. This is a common situation because a chairperson who was a former CEO of the same company is not always well received by the new CEO. However, it is not unusual that these chairpersons have difficulties in letting go of the reins and interfere too much with the CEO's role. In this case, being aware of how a former role influences a current perspective on a new one would be beneficial to both parties.

In my interviews, one-third of leaders (mostly CEOs but also chairpersons) made similar statements on this type of role shift: "Having the ex-CEO as chairperson of the same company is a no-go"; "She cannot let go"; "He always interferes with the daily business"; "It is not that he interferes but that he knows so/too much."

EXAMPLE #5: GORHAM AND MOLLY

Molly was excited to start her new job as CEO. Her chairperson, Gorham, was very experienced and gave her room to do her job. There was just one thing that kept bothering her. Each time they had a meeting or she sat in on a board meeting, she wasn't able to think clearly and would freeze up. Then she would start to sweat. Deep down, she had a feeling that she could never do everything right in Gorham's eyes. She would try harder, but he didn't seem to acknowledge her extra efforts. While he wasn't vocal in a negative way, he never praised her either.

What Molly had yet to realize was that Gorham unconsciously reminded her of her father. They both wore moustaches and had the same way of furrowing their brows and sitting with their arms crossed. Whatever Molly did, it was never good enough for her father. He would always say, "You can do better. I know that you have more potential." She adored her father but felt immense pressure to please him. Her father never acted the same way with her two-years-younger brother, who was a bit of a rebel and didn't seem to care for order or rules.

Had Molly realized that Gorham was having this unconscious effect on her, she could have brought it into her consciousness, seen how her behavior patterns were no longer productive, and taken action to refocus and be more confident in her work and accomplishments. She could have consciously used her energy on her work instead of unconsciously trying to please her chairperson.

A SLIPPERY SLOPE

Conflict generally starts with something small and then snowballs into something so large that it is almost impossible to stop. For example, one person might blow off another person at a board meeting. Perhaps a CEO tells the chairperson and the board about a crisis in one of the subsidiaries that needs a bigger budget. Knowing the chairperson would be reluctant to support it, the CEO withholds the information until a meeting. The chairperson gets upset because the CEO withheld information, and he begins to question the CEO's actions and whether there was a hidden agenda. At the next one-on-one meeting, the CEO takes the better seat in the room and gives the chairperson the seat with his back to the door. The meeting gets emotional, and the CEO feels the chairperson's temper rising each time he prods him. Momentum has already built up, and if they do not address the issues they have, this relationship can turn ugly.

What both parties do not realize is that they are letting their lives be run by insecurities and unconscious drivers of conflict. The CEO does not realize that he does not like the chairperson because he reminds him of his first teacher who oppressed him as a kid. The chairperson feels betrayed because he never expected the CEO to play such power games and is fearful that the CEO might be gunning for his job to dethrone him. What the chairperson does not realize is that he has an unconscious fear that the CEO triggered because he was once dethroned by his younger brother and lost his parents' attention. This makes him feel unworthy, so he unconsciously fights this situation to avoid the dethronement from happening again.

In many cases, this kind of conflict eventually culminates in a showdown of sorts, where the chairperson votes to fire the CEO. The chairperson frames him as a dangerous animal that follows only his own interests and puts power above the good of the company. The CEO gets wind of this and quits before the board of directors can act, then shares his side of the story with his managing team. He even convinces two other people to come with him. The next day, the CEO announces the news about his leaving to the board. The chairperson feels a sense of relief that the CEO is gone, while the CEO feels like he won the game. Both feel like they have won (though deep down possibly having an unpleasant aftertaste) when really nobody is winning because this kind of turnover and toxic environment hinder company culture and productivity. It steers focus away from the business, the clients, the market product, and the employees, all because of a power struggle between two leaders at the top whose job is to lead the company.

FIGHTING THE FIGHT

There's a Maasai proverb that very much applies to the CEO-chairperson conflict:

When the elephants fight, the grass gets trampled.

With the above proverb in mind, it is no surprise that a 2017 Gallup study called "State of the Global Workplace" concluded that 50 percent of employees across all continents have left their jobs to get away from their bosses. The study demonstrated a clear link between employee motivation and efforts, and their relationship with their superiors. Motivated employees are key to driving success in a company, but not when they are getting trampled like grass.

In this same study, Gallup also revealed that only 10 percent of employees fit the description of an engaged employee. This statistic is quite alarming because the economic consequences are approximately $7 trillion lost globally in productivity alone. Reasons for disengagement are usually related to leadership issues such as micromanagement, bullying, conflict avoidance, shirking decision making, stealing rewards of performance, withholding information, blaming, not listening, failing to develop a workforce, and fraud. It all seems like common sense, but conflict at the top is a strong force that distracts from business. If not addressed, it becomes exhausting.

People feel the consequences of compounded drivers of conflict, and work environments become toxic.

The good news is that co-leaders and their organizations can get a handle on this pattern of compounding conflict drivers. In the next part of the book, you'll discover the tools to reverse the toxic spiral and improve your entire organization by cultivating a high-functioning co-leader relationship.

PART III

THE TOOLS TO PREVENT AND MITIGATE CONFLICT

CHAPTER 7

IMPROVE SELF-AWARENESS

Claude is a chairperson who frequently found himself getting into power games with his CEO, Robin. He always thought it was Robin's fault that the conflicts began, but thanks to coaching, Claude began to realize that when he fought with his CEO, some of the fault actually lay with him.

Through developing self-awareness and examining the influences created in his upbringing, Claude was able to pinpoint his drivers of conflict. As the oldest of three kids, Claude experienced a dramatic shift in his childhood relationship with his parents when his second-born brother almost died as a baby. This sudden shift in attention bred a feeling of neglect in Claude. And coaching helped him realize that he still resented his brother for it.

Claude realized that when he was blaming his CEO and trying to wield more power over her, he was actually still fighting with his younger brother in an attempt to reclaim the firstborn position. By bringing this unconscious behavior to his conscious mind, he was empowered to recognize the unproductive pattern it created. This empowered him to overcome and change his behavior pattern.

Even though the experience of acquiring this new self-awareness was quite eye-opening for him, he didn't immediately tell Robin about it. Instead, he began to work on overcoming his drivers of conflict in an effort to change his behavior pattern. Right away, he noticed that Robin started to react to him differently. Their relationship began to improve as they started to build trust with each other.

Claude also became more aware of the patterns in Robin's behavior. For example, Robin consistently had a negative, emotional reaction to feedback—her temper would rise immediately at any hint of criticism. In hopes of improving their relationship even more, Claude shared his coaching experience with Robin, and this convinced her to seek it out for herself. With both Claude and Robin receiving coaching, they built even more trust between them and were able to work consciously toward a high-functioning CEO/chairperson relationship.

It is worth mentioning that Claude's increased self-awareness not only improved his relationship with his CEO, but also his relationship with his wife and children. When he noticed his firstborn son acting out when his younger sister was born, Claude made it a point to act with his boy in a way that helped prevent the same fracture he had felt between himself and his younger brother. Through developing his own self-awareness, Claude was able to help others in his life develop this as well, thus fostering optimum functionality in his relationships.

TOOLS TO IMPROVE SELF-AWARENESS

As discussed in the previous chapter, self-awareness is more than simply realizing that an issue or behavior pattern exists. Once a person becomes aware of an issue, brings it into their conscious mind, and has the story for why the issue has arisen, they must try to dive a little deeper into it.

COACHING

One tool for doing this is coaching, which served Claude and Robin so well. Compared to other disciplines, coaching is a relatively young field, but it has gained strong popularity in the past decade. Many researchers have found that coaching significantly helps leaders become better and more effective. Therefore, investing in a good coach is a worthwhile endeavor.

It is important to distinguish coaching from consulting, since the value they provide is different. While consulting tends toward offering solutions to problems, coaching focuses on helping individuals explore their specific context to find their own solutions so that they can achieve personal, meaningful, and fulfilling results.

In general, living and undergoing an experience that leads to an epiphany is more powerful than being given an answer. For this reason, it becomes the coach's task to help the individual leader discover and access any dysfunctional dispositions they might have. There is no judgment on these dispositions—every individual has them as part of their personality—but having them exposed raises self-awareness to a tremendous degree.

With these dispositions uncovered, coaches use their large toolbox to help a leader correct their flawed perceptions of the self and of their environment in order to boost self-awareness and emotional intelligence. They then work with leaders to identify and agree on strategies and action plans to overcome patterns and rebuild the competencies that are being requested of them.

John Russell, former managing director of Harley-Davidson Europe, Ltd., would agree: "I never cease to be amazed at the power of the coaching process to draw out the skills or talent that was previously hidden within an individual, and which invariably finds a way to solve a problem previously thought unsolvable."[11]

Inevitably, some people will resist coaching. If a person isn't ready, it might be hard for them to be open to self-discovery and improvement. But companies are moving in the direction where coaching is becoming more commonplace, even welcomed. Whereas personal improvement and coaching might have been underestimated or even neglected in a previous era, today it is more likely that a CEO or chairperson who resists coaching might be viewed in a more negative light, because why would they be against learning how to improve?

While one-on-one coaching is effective, combining it with group coaching often is even more effective. Changes in leadership behavior tend to be even longer-lasting when they are brought about in a group setting. Whether it is with a management team or a board, group coaching brings an increase in accountability and trust, especially in the midst of resolving conflicts.

One crucial skill fostered by group coaching is becoming a better listener, something that many leaders lack. By learning to listen, they learn to exercise understanding rather than being defensive or domineering. This change in approach builds trust and motivation among their colleagues, which in turn makes the leader feel more understood and valued.

Furthermore, in groups people tend to take on similar roles that they have in their family; this helps them recognize their default roles faster. The mediators, the clowns, the cheerleaders, and the scapegoats all come to the surface, allowing everyone to recognize patterns of behavior in themselves and others.

Whether seeking a coach for one-on-one or group work, it's important to choose wisely. After all, everyone a person encounters in their life has some sort of personal or professional bias; a coach is probably one of the only unbiased sounding boards that someone can have. Since "coach" is not a protected occupational title, a lot of people claim to be coaches, but for business leaders, it might be best to seek professionals with business experience. Like any other job, a real coach has a certain box of tools with which they can work. And for those who are hesitant, it is good to keep in mind that it is in a human being's nature to seek ways to progress and develop. A coach is there to help unlock a person's potential so they can live a fuller, richer life.

American singer and songwriter Gerard Way once said, "One day, your life will flash before your eyes. Make sure it is worth watching."[12] This statement rings especially true when you consider it alongside the well-known book *The Top Five Regrets of the Dying*, written by nurse Bronnie Ware, who asked people on their deathbeds about their five biggest regrets. Consistently at the top were oft-repeated wishes that they had had the courage to live their life more according to what felt good to them, not just to please others or fit into society's mold, to not have worked so hard, to express feelings, and to let themselves be happier. Many leaders spend too much of their time nurturing or fighting egos or trying to prove themselves to others. They forget what they are living for.

REFLECTION TIME

Another tool for cultivating self-awareness is reflection. It is imperative to take the time to look at the behavior pattern and flesh out your understanding of what you are really doing. Ask yourself, *Where is this behavior really directed? How is this pattern affecting me and others? Why am I motivated to do things this way? How has my upbringing shaped me?*

No athlete—even at the most elite level—exercises twelve hours a day. Every single one of them schedules time for breaks in their training in order to physically and mentally recover. However, it is far too common for top executives to expect twelve, fourteen, or even sixteen hours of "practice" (i.e., work) every day. They schedule back-to-back meetings; they work morning to evening, rushing from one task to the next, without even taking ten minutes to step back and look at the big picture. If there are no meetings planned, they check emails, texts, chats, or pick up the phone just to keep themselves busy, not realizing the danger of becoming overloaded with information. As a result, they become more deeply entrenched in their current patterns of behavior, acting on ingrained impulses without evaluating whether they are truly helpful. They also become further disconnected from their deepest feelings and needs. Like so many of us, they live in this hyperturbulent world that leaves them with little to no time to look inside and consider whether they are really happy or fulfilled. They get so busy making a living that they forget to make a life.

Remember Carsten, former CEO of Swisscom, who complained that he had hardly any time windows within which he was free from professional and personal commitments. He added that each person needed such time windows; otherwise, one hurries from commitment to commitment without room to breathe.

Reflection time is not simply taking time to think. Thinking is for generating new ideas and plans or weighing a complex issue to reach a decision. It is a rational exercise done amid the specifics of a given situation. In contrast, reflection happens when you step outside the situation and look at it from another perspective, much like an actor pausing a scene, stepping off the stage, and seeing how the scene reads from the balcony. Reflection asks less *what* your rational mind thinks and more about the inner thoughts, feelings, or emotions that influence *how* you think.

Reflection is a practice characteristic of leaders with a strong and healthy sense of identity. By fostering skill and flexibility in dealing with the ambiguity that leadership brings—the moving back and forth between thinking, reflection, and action—reflection guards a leader against impulsive and emotional responses, pathological behaviors, and misuse of power.

If you want to perform at the top level, it is important that you schedule breaks for your mental and emotional recovery to take place. Rather than holding meetings back-to-back, you must give yourself time in between to reflect on your feelings about the meeting you just had and about the one that you'll attend next. Staying busy gives the illusion of control, but it is really in those moments of personal reflection that you maintain control of your leadership role by reconnecting with your emotions, values, and unconscious drivers of behavior. As Confucius wrote, "Learning without reflection is a waste; reflection without learning is dangerous."[13]

STILLING THE BUSY MIND

One of the greatest challenges to self-awareness is the difficulty of focusing on a quiet inner journey in the midst of a noisy outer world. Another helpful tool for improving self-awareness is meditation, a practice that focuses on the interactions of the body, mind, brain, and behavior. Meditation, like coaching, has quietly made its way into corporate life. Its long history of use underscores its potential to increase calmness and physical relaxation, enhance psychological balance, cope with illness, and improve overall health and well-being.

Although many different types of meditation are known, most of them share the following aspects:

- A location that is quiet and allows for minimum distractions
- A posture that is comfortable (sitting, lying down, walking, or other)
- A focus of attention (to a set of words, an object, or one's own breath)
- An open attitude toward it (no judgment, even if distractions occur)

Traditional meditation modalities are not the only way to experience the benefits of this practice. In other words, it is not necessary to be the type of person who finds pleasure sitting cross-legged on the floor. There are many other options for quieting your mind for a few minutes through stillness and relaxation. For some, this is best achieved by sitting in nature, listening to relaxing music, looking at the flame of a candle for a few minutes, or even just taking a few deep breaths. Others find it easier to enter a meditative state through repetitive activity such as walking, running, cycling, or working in their garden. The goal is to reach a place of inner stillness, in contrast to life's constantly moving hamster wheel, and to resist trying to order one's thoughts in favor of simply receiving them and then letting them go.

Leaders such as Ford Motor Company executive chairperson Bill Ford Jr., former McKinsey managing partner Michael Rennie, former Swiss National Bank head Philipp Hildebrand, former International Monetary Fund chief legal counsel Sean Hagan, and many others swear by meditation and its benefits. Bridgewater founder Ray Dalio has been practicing meditation since 1969. They claim it increases focus, stops confirmation bias, and helps them pull back to see the bigger picture and find a greater sense of serenity. For this same reason, a large number of major companies—Procter & Gamble, Unilever, Nortel, Comcast, Pixar, and many more—have introduced meditation or decompression time into their company cultures to encourage creativity and a "work smarter, not harder" approach.

BREAKING THE BUSYNESS ADDICTION

Most of us were trained from an early age to stay busy. For example, how many parents and teachers do you know who proclaim that doing nothing is a good thing? By the time we reach adulthood, the unconscious mind insists that busyness is good and inactivity is laziness, irresponsible, and a waste of time. This is why people feel guilty when they are not active, even during weekends or moments between appointments. Hardly anyone espouses the benefit of taking a few moments for pause and reflection at work; if anything, it is the opposite that is considered good form. In today's world, being busy is synonymous with being effective.

Being busy can even provide a temporary buzz to the brain. Checking cell phones, laptops, tablets, and so forth sends a chemical to the brain in the form of dopamine, creating a rush through the bloodstream that isn't easy to stop. It makes busyness almost addictive. It is not a coincidence that as access to information and entertainment increases, so does the rate of burnout and stress disorders.

> Neuroscientists have found that when a task is performed, the left side of the brain processes the majority of the logical and sequential information, and the right side processes visual information intuitively and holistically. The right side gets stimulated in times of calm, while the left side is an ally of busyness and tends to override the right side.

What people fail to recognize is that this busyness only gives the illusion of control; oftentimes, it is also a defense mechanism. It masks the demons that haunt people, such as loneliness, fear, depression, and worthlessness. In providing an escape from uncomfortable feelings, busyness makes people lose touch with both themselves and others. They alienate themselves from their feelings and needs, and they lose touch with who they are.

It is crucial to realize that bringing those uncomfortable thoughts into the conscious mind can be fruitful and far more rewarding than focusing on solving issues for the sake of being busy. That's why part of staying physically and mentally healthy is including downtime in your life.

In order to explore your inner world and activate your own inner resources, it is crucial to balance activity with inactivity, noise with quiet. Good leaders are the ones who balance action and reflection. They make space for downtime, which helps them come to important insights.

A lot of processes remain unconscious for a while before they enter into consciousness. For example, a lot of people have insights or new ideas in the shower, in the car, when they lie down, or when they travel. This is called the alpha state, where routine activities are absent, and daydreaming and mindfulness emerge. In this state, people also tend to see decreases in confirmation bias.

For this reason, a lot of newer companies and startups have incorporated downtime into their business models, not just in the interest of their employees, but also to encourage the development of their brand. Along with encouraging breaks throughout the day, companies such as Facebook, Google, Pinterest, Dropbox, Eventbrite, Airbnb, and Twitter offer benefits calculated to avoid the counterproductive mental and physical health issues that spring from employees whose minds are always spinning. These benefits include yoga and Pilates classes, massage therapy, open vacation policies, and sometimes even yearly budgets to travel anywhere in the world.

For top executives, taking a vacation or a sabbatical is vital to being an effective leader over the long term. As most of our behavior is automatic and repetitive, the new and unexpected are powerful triggers for self-reflection and encouraging change. Disconnecting from work to do something that helps you relax and takes your mind away from the quotidian can help you progress mentally by putting you in a more peaceful mental state.

GETTING STARTED

One way of starting your journey toward greater self-awareness is finding a coach. Coaches are usually best found by word-of-mouth recommendation. If a friend or someone you trust has a coach, start by asking them about their experience. You can also reach out to the author of a good leadership development book and ask if they offer coaching or if they can recommend someone who does.

To get the best results from your coaching experience, however, it is important to ensure that the coach you choose is a good fit with you. One aspect of that fit is expertise. It is imperative that coaches for higher-level leaders have some sort of background and experience in business, as they are more likely to understand dynamics, organizational life, hierarchy structures, and power games.

Another important aspect of finding a coach is good chemistry between you. Fortunately, most coaches make it easy to test this dynamic by offering informal initial meetings. This is as much to the coach's benefit as the client's—after all, the relationship is a two-way street, and the coach has to want to work with the client, too.

While you are seeking out the right coach, though, there's no need to wait on developing self-awareness. Quite the contrary. You can begin helping yourself immediately through a variety of techniques and tools.

JOHARI WINDOW

A widely known technique for improving self-awareness is called the Johari window. It is a communication model that helps with the analysis of interpersonal communication—how it is provided and received. Invented by American psychologists Dr. Joseph Luft and Dr. Harry Ingham, it consists of a grid divided into four quadrants. Each of those quadrants stands for a type of communication exchange.

The upper-left quadrant is the open area, meaning the awareness of the impact of your communication on others and others on you. If this area is very high, chances for running into conflicts are minimized.

In the upper-right corner is the blind area, which is a lack of self-awareness of the impact you have on others, but awareness of the impact others have on you. This area can lead to an ignorance about yourself. Seeking feedback can help expand the open area.

The lower-left corner is called the hidden area, which indicates awareness of the impact you have on others but not the impact others have on you. This area can lead to defensive behavior and an increased chance of interpersonal conflicts. Disclosing and exposing information and feelings can help reduce the hidden area.

The lower-right corner is called the unknown area. This

area is a lack of self-awareness as well as lack of aware-ness or understanding of others with respect to feelings, behavior, and capabilities (on the surface or even deeper). People with little or no experience or with a low self-belief are expected to have a larger unknown area. This area can be reduced through self-discovery, observation by others, or coaching.

This grid serves as a guide for figuring out which way you need and want to move. You can test it out with close family and friends to see what perceptions of you exist and how that differs from how you perceive yourself.

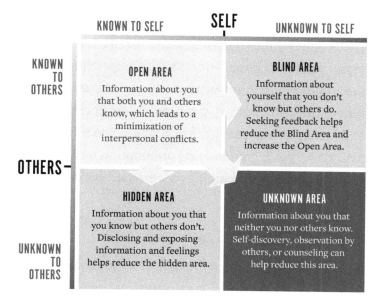

JOHARI WINDOW

	SELF	
	KNOWN TO SELF	UNKNOWN TO SELF
KNOWN TO OTHERS	**OPEN AREA** Information about you that both you and others know, which leads to a minimization of interpersonal conflicts.	**BLIND AREA** Information about yourself that you don't know but others do. Seeking feedback helps reduce the Blind Area and increase the Open Area.
UNKNOWN TO OTHERS	**HIDDEN AREA** Information about you that you know but others don't. Disclosing and exposing information and feelings helps reduce the hidden area.	**UNKNOWN AREA** Information about you that neither you nor others know. Self-discovery, observation by others, or counseling can help reduce this area.

OTHERS

HIDDEN COMPETING COMMITMENTS EXERCISE

This exercise is very beneficial for learning to embrace change. In general, change triggers uncertainty. It is not necessarily the change that people oppose but the fear of the loss that comes with change. Often, people are stuck in their hearts, not in their minds. Whether the fear is real or not, the loss or potential for loss is real. This is why people prefer to stick to what they know and resist the unknown. It is a defense mechanism that hinders all of us from letting go of the stable image we hold of ourselves.

Organizational psychologists and researchers Dr. Robert Kegan and Dr. Lisa L. Lahey developed a diagnostic test for immunity to change. It is a four-stage process that supports people in discovering hindering blocks of change.

The first step steers individuals to a list of questions that highlights their commitments and prompts them to pick the commitment they want to work on. The second step is to identify the competing commitments (their behavior and feelings) that work against change. The third step is to uncover the big underlying assumption tied to them. And the last step is changing the resistant behavior.

COMPETING COMMITMENTS CASE STUDY: MITCH

To resist change does not mean to consciously oppose or to be inactive. Rather, it means unconsciously holding onto so-called hidden competing commitments, despite a serious willingness to change. Creating self-awareness is the first step in shifting the internal attitude to motivate the actions that support the growth. These small, incremental steps help build "muscles" for powerful shifts in behavior.

Such was the case with Mitch, the CEO of a small company, who came across as solid, strong, and highly self-confident and rose naturally to positions of power (e.g., other CEO or board positions). However, he found himself often shying away from taking ownership of that power and even letting it be taken away from him. Reflection led him to conclude that as a result of shame he had experienced as a child, he unconsciously felt that he didn't deserve power and would be negatively exposed if he failed in using it well.

Determined to conquer his fear of failure, Mitch underwent the Competing Commitments exercise, a systematic approach aligned with the four-step diagnostic test mentioned above.

Selecting One Commitment to Change

Mitch engaged with his desired commitment to change by framing it as an active endeavor:

I commit to actively accept, look for, or initiate opportunities to fill my position's shoes (grasp and claim "power") and allow myself to deserve success.

He then turned his focus to examining the competing commitments, the behaviors and feelings that unconsciously competed with the commitment he wished to make.

Examining Competing Commitments

Mitch was doing quite a few things to keep himself from claiming power and potentially failing.

He experienced a competitive and ambitious drive to perform his job well and deliver superior results. At the same time, he felt convinced that he could never reach the mastery level that he had observed as a child in his parents. He feared that he might not be able to live up to the standard of others and that people would lose interest in him or view him as unqualified.

In order to disguise his fear of power, he spoke a lot about his accomplishments or achievements, adopting an uncharacteristic tone and strength of voice and choosing words that didn't seem to fit his usual vocabulary. At the same time, he avoided involvement in organizational politics and power games, fearing they would expose him even more.

While he was thirsty for feedback, he felt uncomfortable and even embarrassed when he received compliments and positive assertions. He believed others were just being kind or that they might not have seen the whole picture. Unwilling to feel like a fraud, he resisted looking for or listening to the feedback that could have bolstered his confidence.

Uncovering the Big Assumption

Mitch's biggest assumption was that he would be left disliked and alone if he claimed power, and even more so if he failed in using it. While he was well aware of the fact that actual chances for him to be left alone were close to zero, he recognized that this unconscious belief prevented him from following through on his commitment.

Action Plan

A series of small, safe, and actionable experiments helped Mitch reach and maintain the commitment to actively seek opportunities to fill these footsteps.

He speaks more about his qualification in his professional sphere. Instead of just sharing "the facts" of his biography while focusing on other people's accomplishments, he created a list of his achievements (there are quite a few of them, indeed) and began to include them without bragging (or allowing himself to feel as though he were bragging).

He asks more often for honest feedback and, when he receives it, stays with it for a moment, resisting the tendency to find arguments against it. When potentially derailing thoughts occur to him, he resists thinking them through to the bitter end.

In conversational settings, he maintains his sincere interest in people by being empathetic, listening well, and asking questions, but is also more proactive in sharing his experiences and opinions, whether he is asked or not.

Impact

The Competing Commitments exercise is a very powerful tool that can be applied to any issue—fear of success, needing to delegate more, becoming a better listener, or any other positive change you wish to create. In applying the exercise step by step, Mitch was rewarded with incremental progress in his thoughts and actions. While there is occasional backlash (when old habits kick in or when he doesn't stick to his action plan), the overall direction is forward and the noticeable progress is nothing short of thrilling for him.

Mitch's progress has also had a positive impact on his

family. Being open with his struggles and his intentions has increased both vulnerability and strength in his family relationships, allowing him to be supported and loved, as well as held accountable to his commitments.

While Mitch has not yet received feedback from his professional sphere, he recognizes that it may well be that he comes across perfectly natural to them. In any case, he enjoys making progress under the radar, which gives him time, space, and focus to continue rewriting his inner script.

As Mitch realized, it is impossible to press a button to change. The process demands trust as well as patience, mainly with oneself but also with others. Change happens not in a single moment of "awakening" but emerges gradually through questioning deeply rooted, long-term psychological beliefs. These beliefs can be painful or embarrassing to confront—this is why some people choose to stick with competing commitments rather than challenge themselves to achieve the change they want to. It is a human impulse to protect the self, but if you desire positive change, it is important to work through these barriers to redefine the beliefs that previously held up your world.

JOURNALING YOUR INNER THEATER

Using a journal is a great way to learn about your inner

landscape. When describing situations, you write down both negative and positive emotions associated with events and then rate them by intensity. By mapping your emotions and rating them, you can identify patterns for strong emotions being triggered or which people trigger which feelings. You try to find links between thoughts, feelings, and bodily sensations and where they stem from. You can then acknowledge them, accept them, and practice letting them go.

The first wave of emotion released is always the strongest. For example, imagine you see an email from your chairperson and feel a pain in your stomach. Instead of immediately walking away, suppressing, or acting on the emotion—for example, by sending back an emotionally charged response—sit with the emotion and acknowledge it. Usually, the next wave of emotion will not be as strong when the next email comes. It is a small step of connecting with yourself and fostering your own self-awareness.

One helpful exercise in journaling is the adverse event exercise, which prompts you to think about an incident, uncomfortable situation, or event and see how it affects you. It involves sitting back and observing yourself to figure out how and why you are feeling uncomfortable. To do this, you make a list of adverse events and then you try to spot your pattern. For example, you might come to realize you always get upset when stuck in traffic or when employees come in unshaven or unkempt. It is about trying to find patterns in your behavior by reflecting on a series of events and seeing what negative emotions are triggered and where they might originate. This awareness helps you consciously choose your behavior instead of unconsciously acting on your impulses.

SEEKING OUT FEEDBACK FOR A REALITY CHECK

History frequently teaches us that leaders who lack the ability to face a reality check suffer grave consequences. Resisting feedback and the critical self-reflection it brings is an indication of hubris and a weak sense of self—character traits that can likely lead to harming others and eventually themselves.

Historically, the wise fool or jester served the purpose of presenting honest feedback to the king. Today, however, leaders have to find a source of feedback through other means. Some seek it out from employees and colleagues, but sometimes family members and close friends are the ones best suited to this role. They know the leader the best, including their background and upbringing, which means they can offer the most insight into the leader's unconscious drivers and intensifiers. However, the tricky thing with family members and friends is that although they usually are closer to the leader than anybody else and might know them best, the leader's excessive workload often leads them to sacrifice their family, friends, personal needs, and health for the job and the organization. But, as Brigitte Ederer, a former member of Siemens's management board, once put it:

> The move to the top of the corporate pyramid brings changes with it that nobody knows how to deal with. You can no longer ask anybody because with certain decisions, you are the last authority and on your own. You ran the risk of becoming lonely. If you don't take care of your friends, they become fewer and fewer.[14]

It cannot be overstated that all leaders need people at their side whom they can trust and ask for feedback and advice. They need to know that these people will tell them the truth regardless of their status or title, which is not always the case in a business setting.

ENJOY THE JOURNEY

It is important to enjoy the journey toward increased self-awareness and improved self-leadership. It is not always easy or comfortable, but what it yields in personal growth is much more significant than you can conceive of. Seeking a coach is always a wise move. But you can employ the tools discussed in this chapter before you do. Also, there are numerous personality tests out there that help you get to know yourself better. By seeking to improve yourself, you are already putting yourself ahead. After all is said and done, there is nothing to lose in trying.

CHAPTER 8

CREATE A COLLABORATION CONTRACT

The majority of CEO/chairperson relationships do not work well, but that does not have to be the case. Leaders in these roles do not operate in a black box—there are tools and means to help improve their relationship. The question then becomes, why wouldn't they improve their relationship and company culture? Without an improvement, there is a lot to lose. More importantly, however, this improvement offers so much to gain.

Take Mary and John, a chairperson and CEO, respectively, who had a rather pragmatic relationship. While there were no open conflicts between them nor had they ever fought, they weren't overly trusting of each other. Both harbored a certain uneasiness about the other—a suspicion that the other was trying to fish in their pond.

Both Mary and John felt they understood their roles because they were described in the organizational rules and functional chart, yet each had a different understanding of turf. This different understanding generated a power game that always hovered over them with the potential to disrupt the tenuous trust between them. This bothered them both, but they didn't know how to go about addressing it. Instead, they kept each other at a professional distance. They would discuss strictly necessary business matters, mostly on the phone, but never anything even remotely personal.

Mary was referred to my coaching by one of my clients, the CEO of another company. This client shared with Mary about the importance of the conscious and unconscious drivers of conflict and their intensifiers. This inspired Mary to examine the impact her own family origins had had on her. In self-reflecting, she became aware of how much she had been marked by her family dynamic and birth order. She learned she was a functional firstborn. She had never considered the possibility but detected the telltale behavior patterns and characteristics in the way she was brought up. As so often happens, Mary's newfound self-awareness helped her recognize some of these same behaviors in her CEO—she speculated how he, too, must have been impacted by his family dynamic and maybe life-changing incidents.

Mary's friend also told her about the Chairperson-CEO Collaboration Contract (CCCC) she had created with her chairperson. When Mary reviewed the CCCC, she wasn't sure about being able to discuss it through with her own CEO. However, she knew their relationship needed a boost and feared how a potential power struggle might affect her workforce if she didn't take action to change it.

Dr. Philippe Hertig, a partner at the leading executive search firm Egon Zehnder International, told Swiss business newspaper *NZZ* that "50 percent of a company's success depends on the relationship between the chairperson and the CEO."[15] The risk of not getting the relationship right is too great to just sit back and ignore. As Mary rightly concluded, the only harm would be in not trying. Accordingly, she approached John, explained the potential benefits of a CCCC, and suggested they discuss one.

DEFINING THE CCCC

The CCCC is a type of psychological contract. It is a verbal agreement between two people that can entail a public commitment to employees and other stakeholders.

Thus, it is not something that needs to be signed or written down. Rather, it is a process that is talked through and acknowledged by both parties. Far from being a transactional agreement, the CCCC is a relational contract that is about building trust, reframing instincts, and building a common language between a CEO and a chairperson.

A full version of the CCCC can be found by visiting www.chairpersonceocollaborationcontract.com.

As we discussed in chapter 1, a psychological contract is unconscious, influenced by someone's upbringing and past experience. It is developed less by conscious thought processes and more by a person's needs.

In the same way, a CCCC is less rational and more relational, which makes it by nature more subjective, longer term, and broader in scope. It consists of interpretations of promissory obligations, which means that interpretations are divergent. It establishes role clarity by focusing on the how instead of on the what. It involves talking through the many elements of roles with your co-leader with the goal of improving communication and role clarity. This, in turn, helps reestablish and nurture trust to foster a healthier work environment and improve productivity.

The CCCC asks for high personal commitments. For this reason, the content of the contract should be framed to avoid contract breach by influencing each party's perception of the other's behavior. According to Denise Rousseau, two key conditions that lead to trust are judgment of integrity and belief in benevolence. The more trust between the two parties, the less likely a breach of the CCCC because trust serves as a guideline that influences a person's interpretation of the other's behavior.

Executive co-leaders embarking on the CCCC must commit to the following:

- Strict confidentiality
- Neutral environment
- An oral discussion format (as opposed to a written format, which creates a transactional atmosphere)
- A set number/frequency of meetings
- Common goals
- Agreement on output (e.g., whether to share results with the board of directors, how to proceed in their relationship should the process be interrupted, etc.)

DISCUSSING THE CCCC

John was rather skeptical about the proposal of discussing the CCCC, given that Mary was his boss. He suspected that it might be something she would use to impose her opinion on him. He voiced this reservation, to which Mary responded by suggesting they hire a facilitator to guide them through the process. John agreed, provided that they both be involved in choosing the moderator.

They approached me, and I led them through a process of three sessions, the first of which proved to be rather demanding for both of them. They had to open up about themselves and answer questions such as "What does power mean to you?" and "How do you define trust?" Initially, both Mary and John fell back on their defense mechanisms. I helped them navigate through the discomfort of being more vulnerable with each other.

> An excessively personal discussion is not the goal here. Rather, the goal is for co-leaders to share a more human side of themselves for the sake of improved mutual understanding and increased trust.

As the saying goes, the first cut is the deepest. By the next session, both Mary and John started to enjoy the conversations without feeling too exposed in front of the other. They saw how being open with each other bonded them, creating a mutual trust that greatly improved their relationship. With this trust, they could more clearly assume their roles and see what expectations to have of each other.

By the final coaching session, Mary and John agreed that despite the confidentiality agreement and the non-signing nature of the contract, they wanted to share with their team members and other stakeholders that they had completed the process. They even agreed to share some of the outcome. Having both learned so much valuable information about the other's viewpoint, expectations, and values, they worked together to redefine their job descriptions. They both felt liberated in their roles and found the process had boosted their energy, helping them focus on their jobs, employees, and clients more. John even reported that he was approached by a couple of people on his management team who had noticed his improved relationship with Mary. Once those people learned about the CCCC, they wanted to engage in the process with some of the members of their respective teams. The desire for improvement became infectious in the company.

LEADING THE CONVERSATION

When I sit down with a CEO and chairperson for the first time to help them negotiate a CCCC, I first ask them to describe their relationship, how they feel about it, and what motivates them to discuss a CCCC. I also ask them to visualize their ideal outcome and what this outcome would lead to.

After explaining my experience as a CCCC facilitator, I emphasize the importance of the CEO/chairperson relationship. I address the fact that their relationship is likely to span a long time—that a CCCC isn't a quick fix. They need to decide how long and where they want to spend their time together going forward, whether that's in a neutral location at the office or over lunch, dinner, or a drink.

I begin the discussion around conscious and unconscious elements of personality and behavior before moving into interpretations of and perspectives on trust and what it means to both individuals.

CONSCIOUS DRIVERS
Trust

- How do you define trust? What does trust mean to you?
- How do you grant trust? Do you tend to give the benefit of the doubt, or do you harbor initial mistrust that improves with positive results?
- How would you describe the level of trust between you?
- How are you going to increase and nurture trust in your relationship?

Role Clarity

- Is there clarity about each of your roles?
- Have you ever discussed in depth how the chairperson and CEO roles should be filled?
- Is there a role history that influences role misinterpretations?
- How will you address and discuss future issues and misunderstandings?

- Going forward, whose job will it be to ensure role clarity?

UNCONSCIOUS DRIVERS
Corporate Governance That Is "Lived"

- Discuss the chairperson's role (scope, interfaces, responsibilities, who is in charge of what, when, how).
- Discuss the CEO's role (same as above).
- How aligned are your views, perceptions, and expectations?
- Does your former role influence the perspective of your current role?
- Where are overlaps of responsibilities and how are you going to tackle them?
- Who represents the company when and how? Which potential situations might be critical and might lead to conflicts?

Power

- How do you define power?
- What does power mean to you?
- How would you describe the power balance between you two?
- Going forward, how can you agree to handle the division of power?

Time Spent

- How much time do you spend together and how? Do you perceive it as too little, enough, or too much? Why?
- What would be an ideal frequency and amount of time to spend?
- Going forward, where are you going to spend this time (office vs. neutral location; go for lunch, dinner, a drink, or a hike)?

OTHER

Goals

- What are your goals, professionally and personally? Role clarity seems to increase the (legitimacy of) power to achieve goals. For this, a mutual understanding and alignment of the goals are essential.

Success

- What does success mean to you?

Communication

- How would you describe the nature and quality of the communication between you two?
- Going forward, how will you define and handle communication?

Only after these issues have been fleshed out and talked through do the co-leaders return to the written job description and the organizational rules and charts. With their newly gained insights and mutual trust, they are in a much better place to discuss the details of their roles, responsibilities, and balance of power.

The CCCC does not end here, though. Even with all the progress that has been made, there needs to be time set aside for each person's self-reflection. This happens as a second part of the first session but individually. Content and outcome are not shared. Each leader needs to think deeply about their background, past experiences, and unconscious drivers through questions such as:

- Which authority figure from the past does your counterpart remind you of, if any?
- How has your family and upbringing impacted you?
- Has there been a life-changing incident that has marked you?
- Which values were held high in your family? Do they differ from the ones you hold high and promote today?
- What emotional reactions are you known for? What situations trigger these emotions?
- What was your niche in your family? What role did you play?
- How has your birth order marked you?

- How would you rate your level of self-awareness? Why?
- How can your self-awareness be improved?
- Is reflection part of your routine? How do you reflect, how often, and for how long?

NOT YOUR TYPICAL CONTRACT

But unlike a standard work agreement, the CCCC is not benefited by being written down. If anything, this gives the agreement a transactional veneer that detracts from the entire purpose of forming a new and improved psychological contract between the co-leaders.

I would venture to say that the process of co-leaders thoroughly understanding each other's point of view is even more important than the text of a formal work agreement.

Sir Denys Henderson, the former chairperson of Britain's Imperial Chemical Industries, once said, "The agreement [job description] should be put down in writing and eventually approved by the board. *But* the process of thoroughly understanding each other's viewpoint is more important than the final text."[16]

Henderson also stated, "The success of the nonexecutive-chairman arrangement is heavily dependent on the chairman's relationship with the CEO...And if the relationship does not work, the board of directors and the company are in serious trouble."[17]

When it comes to functionality, productivity, and the long-term benefit to a company, the CCCC is an essential part of forming the chairperson-CEO relationship.

INITIATING DISCUSSION

Ideally, in the future, coaching and facilitating will be a standard part of "lived" corporate governance. In my interviews, the prevalent perception was that it is the chairperson's job to initiate discussions around role clarity. If a CEO wishes to put a CCCC in place but does not want to approach the chairperson directly, it might be a good option for them to go through a more neutral party such as human resources, independent directors of the board, major shareholders, or a common person of trust, as they understand the CEO/chairperson relationship and have a stake in its improvement.

Innate defensiveness can at first make one party suspicious of or resistant to forming a CCCC. But it is important for the person initiating the discussion not to give up if their co-leader is not immediately receptive to the idea. However, if one party refuses to engage no matter how they are encouraged to do so, that might well be a warning. It is a big statement when someone is flat-out uninterested in developing, improving, and growing a relationship, if only for the good of the company.

Whoever initiates the discussion of a CCCC, there's no question that the discussion should be overseen and moderated by an external facilitator. This could be a professional mediator, executive recruiter, executive coach, or an HR director—just about anyone who will not feel any bias toward one party or the other or threaten their job security. In my experience, the best option is to work with a neutral, trained facilitator who is familiar with high-level leaders. They come with a toolbox for dealing with the issues and potential conflicts related to executive environments. It is crucial that both parties trust and feel good about the moderator.

Finally, ensuring strict confidentiality is key. If it helps make the parties more comfortable, they can sign a non-disclosure agreement beforehand. This is another reason why nothing should be written down in these CCCCs. The location of these discussions should be neutral and private—ideally, not in one party's office or a meeting room where business is usually conducted. At the end, parties are free to discuss whether they want to share their process with their colleagues and agree on what to share.

Usually, the CCCC process starts with a two-hour discussion to get all the information on the table. All parties should expect this first meeting to be the most uncomfortable and challenging, as the two co-leaders are attempting to break familiar patterns in their relationship. The facilitator needs to anticipate that both may be defensive and reluctant to be the first to open up; he or she should come prepared to share stories from previous cases (or even stories of their own) in order to establish trust for both co-leaders.

Fortunately, these sessions do get much easier as they go on. As far as number and frequency, it is up to the facilitator, the flow of the conversation, and progress made in each meeting.

As a coach, I consistently remind co-leaders to trust the process and to trust themselves. Feeling uncomfortable at points during the process, or not understanding the point of questions, is completely normal. As long as both parties have a stake in the discussions, neither one will want to be the one to give up or compromise the process. The likelihood of relationship improvement is much higher when both parties are able to press through the discomfort and trust the process.

There is no one right way to carry out the CCCC. The way the contract goes depends on the context and the situation surrounding the relationship between a CEO and chairperson. It is not an exact science because human beings are complex. It is all part of accepting the unfamiliar, trusting the process, and embracing what comes out of it.

CHAPTER 9

ADVICE FOR UNDERSTANDING DIFFERENT BIRTH ORDERS IN THE WORKPLACE

As a chairperson or CEO who is also a functional firstborn, you are special because your birth rank is. Being firstborn has gifted you with many great qualities in addition to your native talents and traits. But as you know, those qualities bring along a lot of pressure with them.

Being firstborn is the toughest job in the family. You are always in the spotlight, serving as an example for everyone else. You were pushed hard—maybe too hard—and grew up internalizing this pressure as standard. All your life, you've been told things such as "You are the older brother now," "Look after your little sister," "We place our hope in you," or "You are our model child." Even today, you still feel responsible for what others say and do. The pressure to be perfect can be unbearable.

Few people know that Leonardo da Vinci, the polymath genius of the sixteenth century, was a discouraged perfectionist. He once said, "I have offended God and mankind because my work didn't reach the quality it should have."[18] Discouraged perfectionists are never satisfied. Healthy perfectionists know satisfaction because they strive for excellence instead of perfectionism; thus, they can forgive themselves when they fall short.

Your distinctive firstborn traits such as a high IQ, determination, reliability, responsibility, logic, and task- and achievement-orientation have helped you rise to the very top. You are a true leader and achiever. Now that you are at the top, this is the time to try to step outside your firstborn role. Contrary to how you were raised, you are not responsible for everybody else. You do not have to try to save the world all on your own. You do not have to be perfect.

Today's role models are not perfectionists. Instead, they allow people to see that they are human. Every leader makes mistakes. But only true leaders admit those mistakes and grow from them.

Think back to your original leaders—your parents. They acted according to what they thought was right, doing the best that they could with their resources, knowledge, and education. But they were not perfect. Like everyone, they were flawed and in need of grace.

Knowing that, it might be time to analyze how well your upbringing has served you. Which of the characteristics you were bred to display are genuinely beneficial, and which ones hinder you today? Likewise, what responsibilities are truly yours versus those that rightfully belong to others? You will serve yourself and your environment better if you stop the power struggle with those who no longer exercise authority over your life.

You now find yourself as a chairperson or CEO. As part of a team, you know that your relationship with your counterpart is crucial for your company's success. There is strong evidence that birth order determines characteristics that influence your relationships with others, especially those with whom you share leadership, so own the helpful ones and overcome the ones that impede you. Do not just talk; communicate. Compromise with your counterpart because they are more like you than you think. Think back to your own childhood and remember how effective it was for you to be encouraged rather than criticized. Imagine the potential if you and your counterpart were to bundle your strengths, shore up your weaknesses, and work side by side toward a common goal.

With that in mind, take off that firstborn hat when you enter the board or management room. Remember, you and your counterpart are likely in the same boat—that is, firstborns or functional firstborns—which means you both tick the same. It also means that neither of you needs to unconsciously prove things to your parents. In business, there are no siblings to take care of, no "hope of the family." Although it might not be easy for you, it is OK to relax a little bit. Give it a try.

Put aside your favorite comparison game. It only leads to power struggles that become exhausting, distracting, and unhealthy. Both you and your counterpart feel the right to assume the number one position, but remember, there are two different leadership positions. This means you are both responsible for each other as well as for the company you lead. Divide tasks and figure out roles together. Reach consensus on who will control what areas and be content with being king or queen over your assigned range.

As you learn to trust and to be trusted, you'll find that it is addictive. So is shared success. There will come a time when you've forgotten where you buried the hatchet or even how to use it, and this will feel good. You'll be happy because work is about more than just being better; it is about the company's people, culture, and performance. You'll sit down with your counterpart and look at how far you've come and see how to conquer the challenges ahead. A problem shared is a problem halved, and shared joy is joy doubled.

Nobody can take your birth order from you. You are and will always be the firstborn. Still, your knowledge of birth order principles will increase your self-awareness. It is the first step toward psychological well-being. Deep down, you feel the truth in these words. You will be resistant to change, but the best time for a fresh start is now. Only you can allow yourself to change for the better. Make balance a keyword in your life. Let go more often, and help your counterpart do the same. Be true leaders, and let people see you are also just humans, a powerful pairing at the top that can make anything happen.

ADVICE FOR WORKING WITH FIRSTBORNS AND FFBS

Learning how firstborns and FFBs tick is helpful not only for firstborns themselves but also for anyone who works with them. While you cannot let them get away with negative habits, it is well worth it to pick your battles wisely. Here are just a few suggestions for making your interaction with an FFB go more smoothly:

- FFBs need to have their attention grabbed immediately. If you are selling an idea or presenting information, be prepared when you show up and get right to the point.

- FFBs like efficiency because they worry about time and their schedule. Focus on nuts and bolts so that you get in and out as quickly as possible. Do not ask too many "why" questions because these are perceived as confrontational and may put the FFB on the defensive. As they are sensitive to criticism, which pushes against their ego, let FFBs know they are in control of their area and do not press them for decisions.

- FFBs are prone to power grabs, so do not take it personally if they demand that you "get to the point" or give you the impression that you're not prepared enough. If you find yourself getting emotional or upset, step back and ask yourself what are your drivers and intensifiers that are causing this? Take it as a learning moment, remembering that other people can serve as mirrors.

- When talking to an FFB, have the courage to admit your own faults and imperfections. You will be surprised how this can help FFBs enter a comfort level where they can learn to forgive themselves for their own faults. By showing that it is OK to be human and imperfect, you will implicitly reassure them that there isn't a parent out there demanding perfection anymore. It communicates that it is safe to make mistakes and grow from them without being judged.

THE FUTURE OF BIRTH ORDER IN BUSINESS

The highest levels of leadership positions have been and still are overwhelmingly held by firstborns and FFBs. Yet with the emergence of new organizational models, boundaryless companies, flat hierarchies, and the demand for new leadership styles, different birth orders might be better suited to fit these new leadership roles. Traditionally, later-born children are better at initiating change and disrupting norms, while middle-borns are good mediators and negotiators. Depending on the needs of a company, the person at the helm might be valued for those qualities.

With the world of business in a constant state of hyperflux, there's a good possibility that later-borns will become more prominent in seats of corporate power. Research points to later-borns being better at innovating and change management. Therefore, in the future, an FFB may be more valued in a role that requires stability.

As families blend and family sizes in the Western world shrink, the proportion of firstborns and only children in nontraditional environments will increase. Traditionally, parents who wanted to have more children but were constrained for some reason applied substantial pressure on their child. With smaller family size becoming more commonplace, the belief is that these firstborns will be raised with less pressure on them.

Every leader comes to their role with a lens on the world shaped by their own perceptions, which are created in large part by birth order. But this lens can be refined over time by the leader's own work in fostering self-awareness for positive change.

Increasing awareness allows people to overcome unproductive patterns and worldviews internalized in their past. As people apply their awareness when raising children, they will nurture better leaders for the future.

CONCLUSION

When asked how they wanted to be remembered, all CEOs and chairpersons interviewed had a clear answer. The answers themselves weren't very surprising. They wanted to be a role model for their kids, a good person, and someone who helps other people develop. What was striking was how clear it was to them that none of their answers involved money, prestige, or power. One leader even quoted Einstein, saying, "Only a life lived for others is a life worthwhile." What they realized was that a person's enduring legacy is what they do for others. It pushed them to think about the person they wanted to be.

Furthermore, a few of them were surprised to realize they were living a life that was not aligned with how they wanted to be remembered. Their postures shrank and their facial expressions revealed an epiphany that was touching to see. At the same time, this reaction served as a trigger for a fresh start. You could see them drawing a line in their mind's eye between their definitions of power and success—and also not wanting to be the "richest person in the graveyard."

Remember, if you're headed in the wrong direction, life considers U-turns to be legal, in all jurisdictions.[19]

—B. T. HENDERSON

BECOMING AWARE MYSELF

In addition to the journey of interviewing leaders, my own experience of acquiring and applying these tools and concepts had a tremendous impact on my personal and professional awareness and development.

Currently, I am not in a typical CEO/chairperson role. On some projects, I serve as the executive leader, while in others, I have a boss and am being led. In both types of roles, I reflect more before I speak or act. I ask if my impulses are being directed by my ego or my true self. I have learned a lot about my patterns, motivators, and drivers, and I have managed to overcome many of the ones that do not benefit me or my team.

It is astonishing to realize how apparently unrelated events can be related and lead to unconscious patterns that are carried further throughout a person's life. I have enjoyed putting together the clues to find out why my perception of the world is as it is, and why I have developed certain patterns in the way I perceive, assess, feel, behave, and take actions. At the same time, I look forward to working on these patterns to prevent their negative consequences.

Of course, having my eyes opened in this way does not mean I always and immediately respond correctly in every aspect. Self-awareness and improvement are a life-long process. The more you become aware, the more you are able to choose whether you want to act the same way you always have or try to be better. You make conscious decisions where you used to act and react unconsciously.

Previously in my career, I was often told that I was too kind or nice and that I didn't fill fully my position's foot-steps. When I tried to adopt a different approach, though, I felt that I was being too harsh or demanding. Today, I feel much more confident in my skin, which has contrib-uted to my physical and psychological health. I feel more relaxed about myself and more resilient with the tasks at hand. Those around me noticed and encouraged this positive change with their feedback. Thus, increasing the awareness of myself and others has had a positive impact on my working relationships as well as on my relation-ships with family and friends.

I realized that my experiences within the leadership tension field were priceless, even if some were indeed painful. What I experienced with my CEO was essential to my growth and development. I could have blamed others for it. I could have become bitter or brittle, and refused to let others get close to me. But that would have been a pity. Had I gone down that path, I would have missed out on important opportunities for growth.

Sometimes the process of working with someone can be challenging, but those challenges support personal development when you choose to embrace the journey. Supposed setbacks can help bring you to a place of positive change. Having experienced this personally and seen it with clients again and again, I can guarantee that this is the path worth choosing.

An unknown source brings it home: "Acknowledging you have areas to work on is not an admission of failure; it is an admission that you have even more potential."

Once you taste meaningful improvement, it is addictive. My self-improvement has motivated me to actively help others, a desire that fuels my practice as a coach and board member and is aligned with how I want to be remembered. Having been on the other side of this leadership tension field, I want to help others embark on the lifelong journey of developing the self, tapping their potential, and experiencing the rewards of growth in the same positive ways that I did. This is a life whose "film" I believe will be worth watching when it flashes by one day.

I have often been asked whether I would have acted differently back then had I known what I know now. It is hard to answer that question. With the knowledge and experience I have today, I would likely not have ended up in that same situation; I would have been able to interpret statements and situations differently, discussed the roles at length, introduced a CCCC, and in case of resistance, hit the emergency brake earlier.

Had I spent more time reflecting back then, it would most likely have increased my self-awareness, which could have led to a different dynamic between my CEO and me. Going even further back, I would have added more layers in the process of interviewing CEO candidates. I would have tried to learn more about what drove them, how reflective they were, and how they might act in challenging situations or deal with a potential failure.

Even today, after all I have learned, the process isn't over. Will I ever understand everything that is happening to me? Will I ever be able to discover and analyze all the events in my life that contributed to who I am today? Most likely not. But will I continue to make progress? Definitely. The primary task is to continue discovering and understanding, while feeling comfortable with not knowing everything and accepting the way life is. Nature demonstrates the beauty of imperfection—no two leaves of the same tree look alike. Who are we to insist differently?

THE BIGGER PICTURE

Companies frequently talk about making the world a better place, but what does that really mean? If we do not have good relationships at the business level, how do we expect to translate our efforts into a big impact? With better relationships in the workplace, goals and values are better served by the business. Employees are able to accomplish more and make a bigger impact.

Playing power games and sustaining conflicts with others is not only exhausting and distracting, but it also causes real suffering for people. It starts as psychological pain, but it can manifest as physical pain. Fear and doubt quickly lead to anxiety, depression, and difficulties at home. Meanwhile, within the workforce, consistently blaming others and shirking responsibility harms a company's culture, which ultimately means lower productivity and performance.

People who claim to enjoy the power games are not being honest with themselves. This can only be a sustainable model for a sociopath. How would a normal human be able to beat back all the negativity and come away unscathed? In the end, you do not want to realize your errors too late in life and regret them. You cannot turn back time.

This book is an opportunity for a fresh start. It is intended to help you become the person you want to be remembered as. Nothing here requires an overnight change—like sport or art, shifting your leadership relationship for the better comes down to daily personal practice. Be patient with yourself. In the beginning, your new discoveries might make you feel as if you were using your car's gas pedal for the very first time—the car jumps, stops, or breaks down before you learn how to handle it smoothly.

Don't let frustration or discomfort dissuade you. Patience and practice will pay off. Trust the process and trust yourself. Channel your firstborn ambition to turn over a new leaf. It is only through your actions that you continue to learn and develop. Your company, your family, and you will benefit from it. Remember, it can be fun. Enjoy the journey.

ACKNOWLEDGMENTS

To my family and friends, for your invaluable and tireless support and encouragement.

To my interview candidates, for your precious trust and inspiring insights.

To my editors and cover designer, for helping turn the manuscript into a book.

To you, dear reader, for trusting that this content will help you and others grow.

ENDNOTES

1. Jörgen Centermann—ABB. (2002). *Bilanz*. Retrieved from https://www.bilanz.ch/people/joergen-centerman-abb

2. Kowalsky, M. (2013). Jürgen Dormann: "CEOs sind gefährliche Tiere." *Bilanz*. Retrieved from https://www.bilanz.ch/gespraech/juergen-dormann-ceos-sind-gefaehrliche-tiere

3. Ibid.

4. Sellers, P. (2002). Something to prove Bob Nardelli was stunned when Jack Welch told him he'd never run GE. "I want an autopsy!" he demanded. *Fortune*. Retrieved from http://archive.fortune.com/magazines/fortune/fortune_archive/2002/06/24/325190/index.htm

5. Grose, M. (2003). *Why first borns rule the world and last borns want to change it.* Rochester, NY: Random House. P. 18.

6. Leman, K. (2009). *Born to win: Keeping your firstborn edge without losing your balance.* Grand Rapids, MI: Baker Publishing. P. 128.

7. Sellers, P. (2002). Something to prove Bob Nardelli was stunned when Jack Welch told him he'd never run GE. "I want an autopsy!" he demanded. *Fortune*. Retrieved from http://archive.fortune.com/magazines/fortune/fortune_archive/2002/06/24/325190/index.htm

8. Kowalsky, M. (2013). Carsten Schloter: Tod eines CEO. *Bilanz*. Retrieved from http://www.bilanz.ch/unternehmen/carsten-schloter-tod-eines-ceo

9. Ibid.

10. Mettler, J. Papi sitzt auf dem hellsten Stern. *Berner Zeitung*. Retrieved from https://www.bernerzeitung.ch/panorama/leute/Papi-sitzt-auf-dem-hellsten-Stern/story/31505679

11. Williams, P., & Anderson, S. K. (2012). *Law and ethics in coaching: How to solve—and avoid—difficult problems in your practice*. Hoboken, NJ: Wiley. P. 7.

12. One day your life will flash before your eyes. Make sure it's worth watching. Retrieved from https://www.azquotes.com/quote/408595

13. Confucius. (n.d.). Learning without reflection is a waste, reflection without learning is dangerous. *Forbes*. Retrieved from https://twitter.com/forbes/status/485434337614397441?lang=de

14. Pletter, R., Teuwsen, P., & Kowitz, D. (2014). Manager unter Druck. *Zeit*. Retrieved from https://www.zeit.de/2014/07/manager-selbstmord/komplettansicht

15. Gratwohl, N. (2018). Wie der Verwaltungsrat dem Chef Paroli bietet. *Neue Zürcher Zeitung*. Retrieved from https://www.nzz.ch/wirtschaft/wie-der-verwaltungsrat-dem-chef-paroli-bietet-ld.1380043

16. Smale, J. G., Patricof, A. J., Henderson, D., Marcus, B., & Johnson, D. W. (1995). Redraw the line between the board and the CEO. *Harvard Business Review*, March–April 1995, pp. 187–212.

17. Ibid.

18. Bigony, C. (2017). A top strategy for CEOs to create intentionally positive organizations. *Huffington Post*. Retrieved from https://www.huffingtonpost.com/entry/a-top-strategy-for-ceos-to-create-intentionally-positive_us_5a0a5ff9e4b060fb7e59d369

19. 55 short inspirational quotes about life lessons and moving on. Retrieved from http://motivationalwizard.com/short-inspirational-quotes-life-lessons/

REFERENCES

Argyris, C. (1960). *Understanding organizational behavior.* Homewood, IL: Dorsey.

Axelrod, S. D. (2012). "Self-awareness": At the interface of executive development and psychoanalytic therapy. *Psychoanalytic Inquiry, 32,* 340–357.

Behera, S. (2013). What is the alpha state of mind? What are its benefits? *Times of India.* Retrieved from https://www.timesofindia.indiatimes.com/What-is-the-alpha-state-of-mind-What-are-its-benefits/articleshow/180546.cms

Berger, J. (2017). *Invisible influence: The hidden forces that shape behavior.* New York, NY: Simon & Schuster.

Bigony, C. (2017). A top strategy for CEOs to create intentionally positive organizations. *Huffington Post.* Retrieved from https://www.huffingtonpost.com/entry/a-top-strategy-for-ceos-to-create-intentionally-positive_us_5a0a5ff9e4b060fb7e59d369

Borwick, I. (2006). *Organizational role analysis: Managing strategic change in business settings.* New York, NY: Karnac.

Burke, P. J., & Stets, J. E. (2009). *Identity theory*. Oxford: Oxford University Press.

Cane, W. (2008). *The birth order book of love: How the #1 personality predictor can help you find "the one."* Philadelphia, PA: Da Capo.

Carette, B., Anseel, F., & Van Yperen, N. W. (2011). Born to learn or born to win? Birth order effects on achievement goals. *Journal of Research in Personality, 45*, 500–503.

Carroll, M. (2008). *The mindful leader: Awakening your natural management skills through mindfulness meditation*. Boston, MA: Shambhala.

Chapman, J., & Long, S. (2009). Role contamination: Is the poison in the person or in the bottle? *Socio-Analysis: The Journal of the Australian Institute of Socio-Analysis, 11*, 53–66.

Confucius. (n.d.). Learning without reflection is a waste, reflection without learning is dangerous. *Forbes*. Retrieved from https://www.twitter.com/forbes/status/485434337614397441?lang=de

Conway, N., & Briner, R. B. (2002). Full-time versus part-time employees: Understanding the links between work status, the psychological contract, and attitudes. *Journal of Vocational Behavior, 61*, 279–301.

Conway, N., & Briner, R. B. (2005). *Understanding psychological contracts at work: A critical evaluation of theory and research*. Oxford, UK: Oxford University Press.

Courtiol, A., Raymond, M., & Faurie, C. (2009). Birth order affects behaviour in the investment game: Firstborns are less trustful and reciprocate less. *Animal Behaviour, 78*(6), 1406–1411.

Creswell, J. W. (2013). *Qualitative inquiry and research design: Choosing among five approaches* (3rd ed.). Thousand Oaks, CA: Sage.

Crotty, M. (1998). *The foundations of social research: Meaning and perspective in the research process.* Thousand Oaks, CA: Sage.

De Haan, E., & Kasozi, A. (2014). *The leadership shadow: How to recognize and avoid derailment, hubris and overdrive.* London, UK: Kogan Page.

Dormann replaces Centerman at ABB. (2002). Retrieved from https://www.swissinfo.ch/eng/ dormann-replaces-centerman-at-abb/2911280

Dunkel, C. S., Harbke, C. R., & Papini, D. R. (2009). Direct and indirect effects of birth order on personality and identity: Support for the null hypothesis. *Journal of Genetic Psychology, 170*(2), 159–175.

Eckstein, D., & Kaufman, J. A. (2012). The role of birth order in personality: An enduring intellectual legacy of Alfred Adler. *Journal of Individual Psychology, 68*(1), 60–74.

Felton, B., & Wong, S. (2014). How to separate the roles of chairman and CEO. *CFO.* Retrieved from http://ww2.cfo.com/risk-compliance/2004/12/ how-to-separate-the-roles-of-chairman-and-ceo/

55 short inspirational quotes about life lessons and moving on. Retrieved from http://motivationalwizard.com/ short-inspirational-quotes-life-lessons/

Giorgi, A. (2009). *The descriptive phenomenological method in psychology: A modified Husserlian approach.* Pittsburgh, PA: Duquesne University Press.

Goleman, D., Boyatzis, R. E., & McKee, A. (2013). *Primal leadership: Unleashing the power of emotional intelligence.* Boston, MA: Harvard Business Review Press.

Goodsell, J. (1988). *Not a good word about anybody.* New York, NY: Ballantine Books.

Gratwohl, N. (2018). Wie der Verwaltungsrat dem Chef Paroli bietet. *Neue Zürcher Zeitung*. Retrieved from https://www.nzz.ch/wirtschaft/ wie-der-verwaltungsrat-dem-chef-paroli-bietet-ld.1380043

Green, Z. G., & Molenkamp, R. J. (2005). *The BART system of group and organizational analysis*. Retrieved from https://www. it.uu.se/edu/course/homepage/projektDV/ht09/bart_green_ molenkamp.pdf

Grinberg, A. (2015). The effect of birth order on occupational choice. *International Atlantic Economic Journal, 43*, 463-476.

Grose, M. (2003). *Why first borns rule the world and last borns want to change it*. Rochester, NY: Random House. P. 18.

Guest, D. E. (1998). Is the psychological contract worth taking seriously? *Journal of Organizational Behavior, 19*, 649-664.

Healey, M. D., & Ellis, B. J. (2007). Birth order, conscientiousness, and openness to experience. Tests of the family-niche model of personality using a within-family methodology. *Evolution and Human Behavior, 28*(1), 55-59.

Helmreich, R., Kuiken, D., & Collins, B. (1968). Effects of stress and birth order on attitude change. *Journal of Personality, 36*(3), 466-473.

Herriot, P., & Pemberton, C. (1997). Facilitating new deals. *Human Resource Management Journal, 7*(1), 45-56.

Herrmann, N. (1997). What is the function of the various brainwaves? *Scientific American*. Retrieved from https://www.scientificamerican.com/article/ what-is-the-function-of-t-1997-12-22/

Isaacson, C. E., Schneider, M., & Schneider, M. F. (2004). *Birth order effect for couples: How birth order affects your relationships— and what you can do about it*. Gloucester, MA: Fair Winds.

Jackson, K. (2010). Global corporate governance: Soft law and reputational accountability. *Brooklyn Journal of International Law, 35*(1), 43–105.

Johari window. (n.d.). Retrieved from http://web.b.ebscohost.com. ezproxy.insead.edu/ehost/detail/detail?vid=11&sid=d985d7c3-0901-4a09-919b-3e6502484002%40sessionmgr103&bdata=Jn NpdGU9ZWhvc3QtbGl2ZQ%3d%3d#AN=26742018&db=bth

Johari window model and free diagrams. (n.d.). Retrieved from https://www.businessballs.com/self-awareness/ johari-window-model-and-free-diagrams-68/

Jörgen Centerman—ABB. (2002). *Bilanz.* Retrieved from https:// www.bilanz.ch/people/joergen-centerman-abb

Kahn, M. S. (2014). *Coaching on the axis: Working with complexity in business and executive coaching.* London, UK: Karnac Books.

Kegan, R., & Lahey, L. (2001). The real reason people won't change. *Harvard Business Review, 79*(10). Retrieved from https://hbr. org/2001/11/the-real-reason-people-wont-change

Kegan, R., Lahey, L., & Riedel, J. (2015). Demystifying change: When developing leaders falter, probe for "hidden commitments." *EgonZehnder.* Retrieved from https://www. egonzehnder.com/insight/demystifying-change

Kets de Vries, M. F. R. (2003). *Leaders, fools and impostors* (rev. ed.). Bloomington, IN: iUniverse.

Kets de Vries, M. F. R. (2005). Leadership group coaching in action: The Zen of creating high performance teams. *Academy of Management Executive, 19*(1). Retrieved from https://journals. aom.org/doi/10.5465/ame.2005.15841953

Kets de Vries, M. F. R. (2006). *The leader on the couch: A clinical approach to changing people and organisations.* San Francisco, CA: Jossey-Bass.

Kets de Vries, M. F. R. (2015). Doing nothing and nothing to do: The hidden value of empty time and boredom. *Organizational Dynamics, 44*(3), 169–175.

Kets de Vries, M. F. R., & Miller, D. (1988). *Unstable at the top.* Boston, MA: Dutton.

Kidder, D. L., & Buchholtz, A. K. (2002). Can excess bring success? CEO compensation and the psychological contract. *Human Resource Management Review, 12,* 599–617.

Kippenberger, T. (1997). The dark side of leadership: What drives people to become leaders? *The Antidote, 2*(3), 11–13.

Kleiner, A. (2010). The thought leader interview: Manfred F. R. Kets de Vries. *Strategy & Business, 59.* Retrieved from https://www.strategy-business.com/article/10209?gko=cbe31

Kluger, J. (2007). The power of birth order. *Time International* (Canada ed.), *170*(18), 32–38.

Korotov, K., Florent-Treacy, E., & Kets de Vries, M. F. R. (2007). *Coach and couch: The psychology of making better leaders.* New York, NY: Palgrave Macmillan.

Kowalsky, M. (2013). Jürgen Dormann: "CEOs sind gefährliche Tiere." *Bilanz.* Retrieved from https://www.bilanz.ch/gespraech/juergen-dormann-ceos-sind-gefaehrliche-tiere

Kowalsky, M. (2013). Carsten Schloter: Tod eines CEO. *Bilanz.* Retrieved from http://www.bilanz.ch/unternehmen/carsten-schloter-tod-eines-ceo

Krauss Whitbourne, S. (2013). Is birth order destiny? *Psychology Today.* Retrieved from https://www.psychologytoday.com/blog/fulfillment-any-age/201305/is-birth-order-destiny

Kristensen, P., & Bjerkedal, T. (2007). Explaining the relation between birth order and intelligence. *Science, 316*(5832). Retrieved from http://science.sciencemag.org/content/316/5832/1717

Langevoort, D. C. (2011). The behavioral economics of mergers and acquisitions. *The Tennessee Journal of Business Law, 12,* 65–79.

Larcker, D. F., & Tayan, B. (2015). Seven myths of boards of directors. *Stanford Closer Look Series.* Retrieved from https://www.gsb.stanford.edu/insights/seven-myths-boards-directors

Larcker, D. F., & Tayan, B. (2016). Chairman and CEO: The controversy over board leadership. *Stanford Closer Look Series at Stanford Graduate School of Business.* Retrieved from https://www.gsb.stanford.edu/sites/gsb/files/publication-pdf/cgri-closer-look-58-independent-chair.pdf

Lavrakas, P. J. (2008). *Encyclopedia of survey research methods.* Thousand Oaks, CA: Sage.

Leman, K. (2001). *Living in a step-family without getting stepped on: Helping your children survive the birth order blender.* Nashville, TN: Thomas Nelson.

Leman, K. (2015). *The birth order book.* Grand Rapids, MI: Revell.

Leman, K. (2009). *Born to win: Keeping your firstborn edge without losing your balance.* Grand Rapids, MI: Baker Publishing. P. 128.

Lesley, S., Martin, L. S., Oades, L., & Caputi, P. (2015). Clients' experiences of intentional personality change coaching. *International Coaching Psychology Review, 10*(1), 94–108.

Long, S. (2015). *The transforming experience framework.* London, UK: Karnac Books.

Long, S., & Harding, W. (2013). *Socioanalytic interviewing.* London, UK: Karnac Books.

Lüpold, M. (2008). *Der Ausbau der "Festung Schweiz": Aktienrecht und Corporate Governance in der Schweiz, 1881–1961* [The expansion of the "Festung Schweiz": Company law and corporate governance in Switzerland, 1881–1961]. Zurich: University of Zurich.

Maccoby, M. (2004). Why people follow the leader: The power of transference. *Harvard Business Review, 82*(9), 76–85.

Mackenzie, M. (2016). *The courage solution: The power of truth telling with your boss, peers, and team.* Austin, TX: Greenleaf Book.

McMartin, J. (2016). *Personality psychology: A student-centered approach.* Thousand Oaks, CA: Sage.

Messieh, N. (2012). *12 tech companies that offer their employees the coolest perks.* Retrieved from https://thenextweb.com/insider/2012/04/09/12-startups-that-offer-their-employees-the-coolest-perks/

Mettler, J. (2013). Papi sitzt auf dem hellsten Stern. *Berner Zeitung.* Retrieved from https://www.bernerzeitung.ch/panorama/leute/Papi-sitzt-auf-dem-hellsten-Stern/story/31505679

Meyer, E. (2014). Navigating the cultural minefield. *Harvard Business Review, 92*(5), 119–123.

Miles, M. B., & Huberman, A. M. (1994). *Qualitative data analysis: An expanded sourcebook* (2nd ed.). Thousand Oaks, CA: Sage.

Miller, R. (2015). Build up trust over time. *Executive Leadership, 30*(4), 3–3.

Möckli, A. (2016). Dass er seine Arbeit nicht weiterführen konnte, traf ihn tief. *Basler Zeitung.* Retrieved from https://bazonline.ch/wirtschaft/dass-er-seine-arbeit-nicht-weiterfuehren-konnte-traf-ihn-tief/story/28635970

Moustakas, C. (1994). *Phenomenological research methods.* Thousand Oaks, CA: Sage.

National Center for Complementary and Integrative Health (NCCIH). (2017). *Meditation: In depth.* Retrieved from https://nccih.nih.gov/health/meditation/overview.htm

Nelson, E., & Hogan, R. (2009). Coaching on the dark side. *International Coaching Psychology Review, 4*(1), 9–21.

Newport, F. (2011). *Americans prefer boys to girls, just as they did in 1941.* Retrieved from https://news.gallup.com/poll/148187/americans-prefer-boys-girls-1941.aspx

One day your life will flash before your eyes. Make sure it's worth watching. Retrieved from https://www.azquotes.com/quote/408595

Pearce, J. L. (1998). Psychological contracts in organizations: Understanding written and unwritten agreements. *Administrative Science Quarterly, 43*(1), 184–186.

Pietkiewicz, I., & Smith, J. A. (2014). A practical guide to using interpretative phenomenological analysis in qualitative research psychology. *Czasopismo Psychologiczne Psychological Journal, 18*(2), 361–369.

Pletter, R., Teuwsen, P., & Kowitz, D. (2014). Manager unter Druck. *Zeit.* Retrieved from https://www.zeit.de/2014/07/manager-selbstmord/komplettansicht

Pollet, T. V., Dijkstra, P., Barelds, D. P. H., & Buunk, A. P. (2010). Birth order and the dominance aspect of extraverstion: Are firstborns more extraverted, in the sense of being dominant, than laterborns? *Journal of Research in Personality, 44,* 742–745.

Raja, U., Johns, G., & Ntalianis, F. (2004). The impact of personality on psychological contracts. *Academy of Management Journal, 47*(3), 350–367.

Rathbone, J. P. (2013). Zen and the art of management. *Financial Times*. Retrieved from https://www.ft.com/content/32e0b9b4-1c5f-11e3-8894-00144feab7de

Robinson, S. L. (1996). Trust and breach of the psychological contract. *Administrative Science Quarterly, 41*, 574–599.

Robinson, S. L., & Rousseau, D. M. (1994). Violating the psychological contract: Not the exception but the norm. *Journal of Organizational Behavior, 15*, 245–259.

Rohrer, J. M., Efloff, B., & Schmukle, S. C. (2015). Examining the effects of birth order on personality. *Proceedings of the National Academy of Sciences of the United States of America, 112*(46), 14224–14229.

Rousseau, D. M. (1989). Psychological and implied contracts in organizations. *Employee Responsibilities and Rights Journal, 2*(2), 121–139.

Schmutz, C. G. (2016). Calida will eine neue Ära einläuten. *Neue Zürcher Zeitung*. Retrieved from http://www.nzz.ch/wirtschaft/calida-will-eine-neue-aera-einlaeuten-1.18717501

Sellers, P. (2002). Something to prove Bob Nardelli was stunned when Jack Welch told him he'd never run GE. "I want an autopsy!" he demanded. *Fortune*. Retrieved from http://archive.fortune.com/magazines/fortune/fortune_archive/2002/06/24/325190/index.htm

Shahnawaz, M. G., & Goswami, K. (2012). Effect of psychological contract violation on organizational commitment, trust and turnover intention in private and public sector Indian organizations. *Vision: The Journal of Business Perspective, 15*(3), 209–217.

Sherman, S., & Hadjian, A. (1995). How tomorrow's leaders are learning their stuff leadership can't be taught, but can be learned. Winning companies are creating programs to help people grow. *Money*. Retrieved from https://www.money.cnn.com/magazines/fortune/fortune_archive/1995/11/27/208026/index.htm

Smale, J. G., Patricof, A. J., Henderson, D., Marcus, B., & Johnson, D. W. (1995). Redraw the line between the board and the CEO. *Harvard Business Review*, March–April 1995, pp. 187–212.

Snell, S. A., Morris, S. S., & Bohlander, G. W. (2015). *Managing human resources*. Boston, MA: Cengage Learning.

Sommer, C. (2010). *Die Treuepflicht des Verwaltungsrats gemäss Art* [The duty of the board of directors in accordance with art] OR *Schweizer Schriften zum Handels- und Wirtschaftsrecht*: Bd. 298 [Swiss writings on the commercial and economic law]. Zürich: Dike.

Stewart, A. E. (2012). Issues in birth order research methodology: Perspectives from individual psychology. *Journal of Individual Psychology*, *68*(1), 75–106.

Sulloway, F. J. (1999). Birth order. In *Encyclopedia of Creativity*. Berkeley: University of California Press.

Tallman, R. R. J., & Bruning, N. S. (2008). Relating employees' psychological contracts to their personality. *Journal of Managerial Psychology*, *23*(6), 688–712.

The Psychological Contract. (n.d.). *Business Balls*. Retrieved from http://www.businessballs.com/psychological-contracts-theory.htm

Thompson, M. G. (2004). *The ethic of honesty: The fundamental rule of psychoanalysis*. Amsterdam: Rodopi.

Todd, J., Friedman, A., & Steele, S. (1993). Birth order and sex of siblings effects on self ratings of interpersonal power: Gender and ethnic differences. *Individual Psychology*, *49*(1), 86–93.

Tomprou, M., & Nikolaou, I. (2011). A model of psychological contract creation upon organizational entry. *Career Development International*, *16*(4), 342–363.

Turner, R. (2008). *Greater expectations: Teaching academic literacy to underrepresented students*. Portland, ME: Stenhouse.

Van de Loo, E., Kamarudin, M., & Winter, J. (2015). *Corporate governance and boards*. Kuala Lumpur: UNIRAZAK.

Van Teijlingen, E. R., & Hundley, V. (2001). The importance of pilot studies. *Social Research Update*, *35*. Retrieved from http://sru.soc.surrey.ac.uk/SRU35.html

Walters, K. (2012). How my cancer changed my view of leadership: McKinsey & Co's Michael Rennie. *SmartCompany*. Retrieved from http://www.smartcompany.com.au/people-human-resources/leadership/how-my-cancer-changed-my-view-of-leadership-mckinsey-a-cos-michael-rennie/

White, J., Campbell, L., Stewart, A. E., Davies, M., & Pilkington, L. (1997). The relationship of psychological birth order to career interest. *Individual Psychology*, *53*(1), 89–104.

Wilkinson, A., & Johnstone, S. (2016). *Encyclopedia of human resource management*. Cheltenham, UK: Edward Elgar.

Williams, P., & Anderson, S. K. (2012). *Law and ethics in coaching: How to solve—and avoid—difficult problems in your practice*. Hoboken, NJ: Wiley. P. 7.

ABOUT THE AUTHOR

 Throughout her career, Isabelle Nüssli's entrepreneurial mindset, strategic focus, and cross-cultural communication have connected her with complex challenges in national and international business leadership. With strengths in business analysis, strategy, risk management, business development, and finance, she has created and led the implementation of projects, programs, processes, and organization restructures.

Isabelle has held senior management positions in Switzerland and abroad. In recent years, she was chairperson of NUSSLI Group, Switzerland, a leading international provider of portable and permanent infrastructures for sport and cultural events, exhibitions, and trade shows, such as World Expositions, the Olympics, and FIFA World Cups. Earlier roles with the company included global key account manager as well as CFO of the US subsidiaries.

In her earlier career, she managed projects, events, and sponsoring for Zurich Insurance Group and led exhibition projects and organization restructuring for two family businesses. Currently, she serves on various boards and committees.

Isabelle earned a master of business administration (MBA) from Kellogg School of Management at Northwestern University, an executive master of European and international business law from the University of St.Gallen (EMBL-HSG), and an executive master in consulting and coaching for change (EMCCC) from INSEAD.

CPSIA information can be obtained
at www.ICGtesting.com
Printed in the USA
BVHW070230201218
536068BV00002B/455/P